JAN 2020

Praise for

CRASH: THE GREAT DEPRESSION AND THE FALL AND RISE OF AMERICA

by Marc Favreau

A New York Public Library Best Book of 2018

A Chicago Public Library Best Book of 2018

A 2018 Booklist Editors' Choice title

An ALSC 2019 Notable title

**A 2019 NCSS/CBC Notable Social Studies
Trade Book for Young People**

"*Crash* does a great job of mixing personal stories with big-picture history, delivering **a compelling narrative about the Great Depression**—and about how Americans' reaction to it changed our country forever."

—STEVE SHEINKIN, NATIONAL BOOK AWARD FINALIST AND
NEWBERY HONOR AUTHOR OF *BOMB* AND *MOST DANGEROUS*

"**In a forceful, fast-paced, and well-informed narrative, Marc Favreau lets readers experience—no, live!—the worst economic collapse in US history**, introducing us to the individuals who suffered through and labored to overcome the financial and social upheaval that was the Great Depression and the remarkable visionaries who rallied a nation against fear, hatred, and divisiveness until a new and stronger America finally emerged.
An impressive and important work."

—JIM MURPHY, TWO-TIME NEWBERY HONOR–
AND ROBERT F. SIBERT AWARD–WINNING AUTHOR OF
AN AMERICAN PLAGUE

"*Crash* is **smart, thorough, visually engaging—and incredibly relevant**. It may be aimed at ages '10 and up' but **I was riveted**—I think people of any age who are interested in understanding American history, especially in order to understand where we are today, will be, too. It's a clear, concise narrative that makes a complicated history accessible without dumbing down or glossing over the nuances of race, class, and gender."

—KATE SCHATZ, *NEW YORK TIMES* BESTSELLING AUTHOR OF *RAD AMERICAN WOMEN A-Z, RAD WOMEN WORLDWIDE,* AND *RAD GIRLS CAN*

"A tale of heroes, villains, and redemption, *Crash* **is the story we should all be reading**—about a time when Americans were knocked down, dusted themselves off, and rebuilt a world that was safer and more secure."

—MICHAEL ERIC DYSON, *NEW YORK TIMES* BESTSELLING AUTHOR OF *TEARS WE CANNOT STOP: A SERMON TO WHITE AMERICA*

"If you want to understand your grandparents' world into which they were born, thus affecting the world into which you were born, **READ THIS!**"

—BILL MOYERS, EMMY AND PEABODY AWARD–WINNING BROADCAST JOURNALIST AND BESTSELLING AUTHOR

"*Crash* **is a fantastic resource** for young readers to understand the decade that defined America. Through portraits of American resilience—from families in the dust bowl struggling to survive to President Franklin Delano Roosevelt, fighting to restore hope and prosperity to an ailing nation— Marc Favreau tells the story of how our country overcame enormous adversity. This is **a compelling portrait of our past that reminds us how we became the nation we are today**."

—CONGRESSWOMAN ROSA DELAURO, D-CONNECTICUT, THIRD DISTRICT, AND AUTHOR OF *THE LEAST AMONG US: WAGING THE BATTLE FOR THE VULNERABLE*

"*Crash* **is a terrific book**, chock-full of personal touches, details, and photographs that bring to life the people who lived through the Great Depression."

—GEORGE O'CONNOR, *NEW YORK TIMES* BESTSELLING AUTHOR OF THE OLYMPIANS GRAPHIC NOVEL SERIES

"Marc Favreau's style **keeps a mammoth story moving,** hitting the major moments of historical importance while taking care to put lesser-known stories into the narrative."

—TANYA LEE STONE, ROBERT F. SIBERT AWARD–WINNING AUTHOR OF *COURAGE HAS NO COLOR* AND *GIRL RISING*

★ "Favreau gives readers **incisive, penetrating,** at times **heartbreaking** prose. **A dynamic read deserving of a wide audience.**"

—*KIRKUS REVIEWS* (STARRED REVIEW)

★ "An **enlightening and very readable** book on a complex historical period."

—*BOOKLIST* (STARRED REVIEW)

★ "Much like Steve Sheinkin did in *Bomb,* Favreau writes in a **clear and relatable** way....This story is far from a slow-moving history book. For readers who think of themselves as history buffs as well as those who just love a thought-provoking story, *Crash* **will deliver on all levels.**"

—*VOYA* (STARRED REVIEW)

"**Engaging and comprehensive.**...Favreau carefully crafts an enjoyable narrative that **vibrantly depicts individual experiences.**"

—*SCHOOL LIBRARY JOURNAL*

MARC FAVREAU

SPIES

THE SECRET SHOWDOWN BETWEEN AMERICA AND RUSSIA

LITTLE, BROWN AND COMPANY
NEW YORK BOSTON

Little, Brown and Company
Hachette Book Group
1290 Avenue of the Americas, New York, NY 10104
Visit us at LBYR.com

First Edition: October 2019

Little, Brown and Company is a division of
Hachette Book Group, Inc. The Little, Brown
name and logo are trademarks of
Hachette Book Group, Inc.

The publisher is not responsible for websites (or their
content) that are not owned by the publisher.

Image credits can be found throughout.

Library of Congress Cataloging-in-Publication Data
Names: Favreau, Marc, 1968– author.
Title: Spies : the secret showdown between America and Russia / Marc Favreau.
Description: First edition. | New York : Little, Brown and Company, 2019. | Includes
bibliographical references.
Identifiers: LCCN 2019005698| ISBN 9780316545921 (hardcover) | ISBN 9780316545884
(ebook) | ISBN 9780316464901 (library edition ebook)
Subjects: LCSH: Spies—United States—History—20th century. | Spies—Soviet Union—
History. | United States. Central Intelligence Agency—History—20th century. |
Soviet Union. Komitet Gosudarstvennoy Bezopasnosti—History. | Espionage,
American—History—20th century. | Espionage, Soviet—History. | United States—
Foreign relations—Soviet Union. | Soviet Union—Foreign relations—United States. |
Cold War.
Classification: LCC UB271.U5 F38 2019 | DDC 327.127304709/045—dc23
LC record available at https://lccn.loc.gov/2019005698

ISBNs: 978-0-316-54592-1 (hardcover), 978-0-316-54588-4 (ebook)

Printed in the United States of America

LSC-C

10 9 8 7 6 5 4 3 2 1

★ ★ ★

For my co-conspirators:
Patty, Owen, and Emmett

CONTENTS

★

SEEING GHOSTS

O ne morning in the spring of 1981, an American spy
went on a family picnic.

It was no ordinary outing.

Five years of planning, millions of dollars spent developing the latest spy gear, and months of careful training
went into making sure that the picnic went off without a
hitch.

The spy, Ken Seacrest, loaded his two children into a
brown-and-tan Volkswagen bus. He carried his backpack,
stuffed as usual with food, water, and children's toys—
everything for a long day in the park. It also contained
something entirely unusual for a family picnic: a $20 mil-
lion wiretapping device, created by Central Intelligence
Agency (CIA) engineers for listening in on the enemy's
innermost secrets.

The spy drove off into the outskirts of Moscow, the
heavily guarded and closely watched capital of the Union of
Soviet Socialist Republics, or USSR—America's archenemy

in the decades-long Cold War between the world's two superpowers. The entire city fell under the command of the Seventh Directorate of the KGB, the USSR's powerful and fearsome spy agency, which kept watch over foreigners and Soviet citizens alike.

Under their armpits, both Seacrest and his wife, who also worked for the CIA, wore special radio receivers that were set to detect a radio frequency used by enemy surveillance teams on the lookout for American spies. The receivers were connected to "induction" antennas that hung around their necks, concealed beneath their clothing. The antennas, in turn, broadcast a signal to tiny receivers in their ears. Hidden in latex, molded to the shape of their earlobes, and colored to match their precise skin tones, the earpieces were completely invisible.

The Seacrests listened for a telltale code: *dvahd-tsaht awdeen*, or "twenty-one." If they heard those Russian words, they would know that an enemy surveillance team had seen them and blown their cover.

Few Americans had ever made it through the Seventh Directorate's net. Ken Seacrest aimed to be one of them.

The KGB watched and followed all US citizens working for the American embassy in Moscow, because, as the Soviets knew, any one of them could be an undercover agent for the CIA. The trick was not to *avoid* surveillance, the CIA learned, because that would only invite more suspicion. Instead, spies such as Ken Seacrest spent months or years creating false identities for themselves. Like actors on a stage, new CIA agents posted to the Soviet Union played carefully crafted roles. In Ken's case, he cultivated an image of an unassuming embassy official, interested in learning about Moscow and raising his children. He went to museums, took long, predictable walks—and enjoyed family picnics. And he always wore a backpack.

Over time, through such innocuous routines, Seacrest accomplished the first part of his mission: lulling KGB surveillance teams into dropping their guard. He appeared to be nothing more than an ordinary man. Beneath that facade, however, this brave spy took the next step toward one of the most difficult assignments of his career.

★　★　★

During World War II, America and the USSR had joined forces to defeat Adolf Hitler. Their victory over Germany's armies brought peace to Europe. But the calm didn't last. In the summer of 1945, as Europeans picked through the rubble of their ruined cities and burned-out farms, Soviet and American soldiers eyed each other warily. These wartime allies stood for opposing worldviews and hostile ideologies, and their recent triumph over Nazism made them less, not more, open to compromise. Soviet Communists saw the West as their prime adversary in the battle to win the hearts and minds of oppressed people everywhere; America viewed Stalin's government as an enemy of democracy. Who would control Europe, they asked, and whose system—democracy or communism—should dominate the world?

These questions would not be answered by the armies that defeated Nazi Germany. In the late 1940s, a new kind of conflict cast a chill over Europe and, eventually, the entire world: the Cold War. The soldiers who fought this war between America and the Soviet Union maneuvered in secret, often alone, working in the shadows of Berlin, Moscow, and Washington. Their weapons were the trade-craft of spies—the dead drop, the brush pass, the one-time pad—and their missions almost always had the same goal: to obtain vital information about the enemy. These secret warriors often wore the clothes of ordinary men and women, deliberately blending into crowds and shunning the attention showered on the heroes of other wars. But their solitary, sometimes-forgotten exploits would help determine the outcome of this very different struggle.

★ ★ ★

In the early 1950s, the Cold War took an unexpectedly lethal turn. A new race to build nuclear weapons pushed America and the Soviet Union toward a standoff that threatened not just the two superpowers but the entire world.

The sheer power of nuclear weapons themselves, any one of which could destroy an entire city, established a new principle for military conflict, dubbed "mutual assured destruction," or "MAD." The MAD principle argued that a first strike against the enemy would almost certainly fail to destroy its entire nuclear arsenal and would lead to an immediate cycle of retaliation. The cycle would then spiral out of control until both nations completely obliterated each other. What's more, the clouds of radioactive material that spread into the atmosphere (known as "nuclear fallout") all but guaranteed that everyone on earth would perish along with the superpowers themselves.

Thus, instead of victory in the traditional sense, America and Russia sought *deterrence* as their strategic goal. The belief was that a nation could *deter* a "first strike," in the parlance of nuclear strategists, by making sure that the enemy understood that their strike would never succeed. And the best way to send this message was by massive and ongoing buildups of their stockpiles of nuclear weapons. Fear, uncertainty, and one-upmanship became key ingredients of this new approach to warfare.

Deterrence implied a kind of balance between the forces of the two superpowers. But the arms race, the ongoing quest by the United States and the USSR to develop new and more powerful nuclear weapons, perpetually upset that balance. Knowing what the enemy was up to became the essential task of America and the Soviet Union—and the key to the world's survival. And that work fell to the masters of the intelligence game, the spies of the CIA and KGB.

In the 1970s, when Ken Seacrest first began his training to join the ranks of America's spies, the pace of the arms race quickened. Both countries deployed new fleets of submarines packed with nuclear missiles. New missile technologies such as the MIRV (or multiple independently targetable reentry vehicle) were capable of showering not one but several nuclear warheads over a target.

And, most ominously of all, in the mid-1970s the Soviet Union showed signs of pulling ahead, upsetting the balance that had kept World War III in check for nearly three decades. Some American leaders asked: *Was Moscow planning a first strike?*

Desperate to learn more, the CIA turned to one of the most expensive pieces of equipment they had ever built. The KH-11 spy satellite cost nearly a billion dollars to manufacture. This highly classified space vehicle could take razor-sharp images and relay them via an electronic signal directly to the Central Intelligence Agency.

The KH-11 soon made a tantalizing discovery.

Photographs transmitted by the spy satellite showed Soviet construction crews digging a twenty-three-mile-long trench near Moscow. Eventually, CIA analysts discovered that the trench connected the Soviet Ministry of Defense with a closely guarded installation on the outskirts of the city: the Krasnaya Pakhra Nuclear Weapons Research Institute.

This was exactly the break America had been looking

for. The trench, the CIA learned, contained special communications cables to carry the latest intelligence about the Soviets' nuclear weapons program.

But there was a catch. Each cable had been encased in lead and was closely monitored by the Seventh Directorate. The Soviets had taken no risks: The trench was designed to keep the CIA away.

If America wanted to understand the USSR's latest ploy in the arms race, they needed someone on the ground, in the Soviet Union itself. A technical team from the CIA and the National Security Agency—the United States' top secret agency responsible for electronic surveillance—quickly got to work on the daunting challenges of designing a device capable of tapping into the Soviet communications cable. CIA analysts soon identified a single manhole, located on Warsaw Boulevard in Moscow, as the best place for an agent to gain access to the trench.

The analysts knew that Soviet engineers had placed sensors and alarms around the whole apparatus. Moreover, the KGB regularly checked the manholes for tampering. So the CIA would have to create a piece of equipment capable of sensing electronic signals without penetrating the cable itself *and* without being detected. Their solution was a small "collar" that could be attached to the cable—but it would have to be placed carefully, and by hand.

On that spring morning in 1981, this was Ken Seacrest's mission.

★ ★ ★

The husband-and-wife spy team kept quiet during the ride. "We wouldn't say much, especially with the kids there," Ken recalled. "They had to be totally unwitting about what was going on."

A brief nod to his wife was a secret signal that Ken was about to set his operation into motion. If Ken did not return by a specific time, she was to gather the children and leave immediately, knowing that her husband had been nabbed by the KGB.

Like most spies in the field, Ken carried no weapon. His carefully chosen disguise was his only protection. After leaving his family on their picnic blanket, Ken slipped into the woods and changed into the drab clothes of an everyday Soviet citizen, an outfit the CIA had pieced together from flea markets and thrift stores all over Eastern Europe.

On his way to the wiretap site, Ken made a surveillance detection run, or SDR, weaving his way through park trails and across city sidewalks, hopping on and off buses, taking note of his surroundings and any suspicious characters.

"You developed an intuition about what was there and what wasn't," he said. "After a while you began to get a feel for these things."

And yet Ken still struggled with what veteran spies

called "seeing ghosts," the psychological habit of believing that you are being watched by the enemy. KGB watchers, Ken knew, were experts at blending into a crowd. Perhaps that woman in the phone booth was photographing him? Or maybe the driver of the passing bus worked for the KGB?

Finally, Ken reached a place on Warsaw Boulevard next to a grove of birch trees. He recognized the spot immediately, even though this was his first time seeing it.

Months of training had led to this moment.

Covert CIA teams had previously photographed the site from every angle. Using these images, engineers at the "Farm," a secret 9,000-acre CIA training facility in Virginia, were able to construct a mock-up of the manhole. Ken and other agents trained and trained until they knew the cramped space by heart.

Ken understood that no level of preparation could eliminate the risk of an operation under such extreme conditions. "The specific manhole eventually selected for an entry point was in the worst possible location," according to one account, "except for the fact it was better than all the others."

Still wearing his backpack, Ken pried open the manhole cover and slipped inside. He could hear the traffic above him, but he remained focused.

For the mission to be successful, Ken had to work quickly and leave no trace of his presence. He kept a checklist of each piece of equipment he carried with him, as anything left behind might alert the KGB to his tampering.

At that moment, in 1981, the Cold War hinged on the calm nerves and training of one American spy, standing knee-deep in chilly water in a Moscow manhole.

★ ★ ★

That evening, the CIA's station chief in Moscow opened the door to his office, which was hidden deep inside the US embassy on Novinskiy Boulevard.

Someone had taped a scrap of paper to the opposite wall, with "#1" written on it in pencil.

That was all the chief needed to know.

The note was a coded message: The spy had completed his mission.

And yet questions swirled around the operation's outcome. Would the wiretap work? And could the United States glean enough intelligence from its $20 million device to head off its Soviet adversary and avert a nuclear war?

An American nuclear test at Bikini Atoll, Micronesia, on July 25, 1946.

US Department of Defense

ENEMIES

1

THE DEFECTOR

On August 6, 1945, an American bomber named *Enola Gay* soared high over the Japanese city of Hiroshima. At exactly 8:15 AM, its bomb doors opened. *Enola Gay*'s aircrew released Little Boy, an atomic weapon whose blast equaled just under 13,000 tons of TNT. The bomb detonated moments later, killing more than 70,000 Japanese people in the explosion and the resulting firestorms, which obliterated an area nearly five miles wide.

News of the atomic bomb quickly reached Joseph Stalin, the supreme ruler of the Soviet Union, at his headquarters in the Kremlin, in Moscow's Red Square. The world's first nuclear attack stunned the Soviet leader, but not out of pity for the Japanese victims. Rather, the shrewd and ruthless dictator immediately grasped the implications of such a powerful weapon.

"Hiroshima has shaken the whole world," Stalin remarked. "The balance has been destroyed."

The United States and the Soviet Union were, officially, allies in August 1945. But their contributions to the war effort were unequal, with Russia paying the heaviest price for Hitler's aggression. In four years of fighting, nearly eight million Soviet soldiers and twenty million civilians died. Much of Russia lay in ruins that summer. More than anything else, Stalin vowed that no invader would ever threaten the motherland again. History had taught him harsh lessons about the countries that lay on Russia's western borders, and he would not make the same mistake twice.

And now America had surprised the world with a weapon that could devastate entire cities in a matter of seconds. It was a deliberate attempt to intimidate him, Stalin believed. Before the rubble of the last war had even been cleared, Stalin feared that a new and ominous threat to Soviet security lay at Russia's doorstep.

"They want to force us to accept their plans on

questions affecting Europe and the world," Stalin declared to his advisers. "Well, that's not going to happen."

It turned out that the Soviet leader had secret weapons of his own. For well over a decade, his spies had been infiltrating the United States, burrowing their way into private companies, schools, laboratories, and even government offices. Information flowed through intricate networks of sympathizers, collaborators, and unwitting helpers—all of it gathered by agents of the Narodnyy Komissariat Vnutrennikh Del (People's Commissariat for Internal Affairs), or NKVD, and transmitted to Moscow in the form of secret, coded communiqués.

Stalin kept watch over friends and enemies alike, listening in on their communications and stealing their closely guarded secrets. The Americans had outmaneuvered him this time, but on that August day in 1945, the Soviet leader began preparing for the next confrontation.

And then, barely a week later, a single rogue agent pulled a thread that threatened to unravel Stalin's carefully woven net.

On August 14, 1945, the very same day that World War II ended, an American citizen and Soviet spy named Elizabeth Bentley cautiously approached the front door of the FBI offices in New Haven, Connecticut. Wild celebrations were breaking out across the country, as Americans everywhere cheered the Allied victory. But for Elizabeth Bentley, the end of the war was the beginning of a terrifying, unknown stage in her life. Her knees were shaking. More than once, she considered turning around. Other defectors—spies who had switched sides—met grisly fates at the hands of NKVD assassins.

If the Russian secret police knew what I was about to do…, she thought, checking the hallway to see if she had been followed.

At last, she opened the door and crossed the threshold— into the hands of the nation's top law-enforcement agency.

"I'd like to see the agent in charge," she said to the receptionist.

Bentley had chosen New Haven over the much larger FBI office near her home in New York City, betting that she could avoid being followed by Russian agents. As an extra measure of precaution, she took the elevator to an office three floors above, then walked down the staircase to the FBI.

She had good reason to be worried. Anatoly Gorsky, the Washington station chief of the NKVD, had recently written to his supervisors in Moscow that, "judging by her behavior, she hasn't betrayed us yet, but we can't rely on her. Unfortunately, she knows too much about us."

Gorsky concluded that, for Bentley, "only one remedy is left—the most drastic one—to get rid of her."

★ ★ ★

Over the course of a two-hour interview, the startled FBI agent could not decide what to make of this strange woman. She let out her story in dribs and drabs. Her motivations were unclear. It took several meetings for her to get up the courage to reveal her whole story—but when she was ready, Elizabeth Bentley unfurled an almost unbelievable account of a massive Soviet espionage ring operating inside the United States. She had no evidence to back up her claims—until one day, she surprised the federal agents by producing an envelope filled with $2,000 in twenty-dollar bills, which Gorsky had handed her only a few weeks earlier.

"Here's some Moscow gold," she announced to her startled interrogators.

★ ★ ★

Bentley's journey to the FBI offices had begun almost ten years earlier.

For someone who would eventually become so completely tangled in a web of espionage intrigue, Bentley entered her adult years alone, a solitary figure looking for companionship and community. She had been born in Massachusetts and was educated at some of America's best schools—a highly intelligent woman who always impressed her teachers with her maturity and cleverness (the Soviets, in fact, nicknamed her *umnitsa*, Russian for "clever girl" or "Miss Wise").

Throughout her life, however, Bentley was unstable, suffering from alcoholism and possibly psychological disorders. Like millions of Americans caught in the Great Depression, she found herself adrift in the early 1930s, working odd jobs and searching for a sense of purpose. She ultimately found what she was looking for—and more still—in the Communist Party of the United States of America, the CPUSA.

Bentley joined at a unique moment in the CPUSA's history, as the Party's popularity soared during the Depression. For the next five years, the CPUSA grew quickly, attracting thousands of new recruits to its promise of building a new kind of society. To these people, capitalism had failed, and ordinary Americans were bearing the brunt of its collapse. In their eyes, the Soviet Union seemed to be a new, more equitable model, a beacon for a more hopeful future. "A new world was coming—and I wanted to be part of it," Elizabeth said in her memoirs.

In 1938, Elizabeth met a man named Timmy, a strongly built Russian immigrant with red hair, blue eyes, and a nearly lifelong commitment to communism. At eight years old, Timmy had distributed illegal communist leaflets in tsarist Russia; as a teen, he survived being executed by firing squad by playing dead on the ground for two days. Later, in the 1920s, he escaped a prison camp in Siberia and made his way to the United States.

Elizabeth fell in love with this mysterious blue-eyed

Russian man. But she would quickly learn that there was even more to Timmy than a lifetime of exploits on behalf of the Soviet Union. For "Timmy" was Jacob Golos, an agent of Stalin's NKVD and "among the cleverest, most mysterious, and most powerful" spies ever to set foot on American soil, according to one historian.

Against his better judgment, Golos found himself returning his apprentice's affections. It was dangerous for a spy handler of his stature to get involved romantically with one of his spies. But Golos (and his superiors in Moscow) also recognized her special value to the Soviet Union. Here was a woman with impeccable Yankee credentials, who had been educated at elite colleges and had few living family members or other attachments. She was the perfect secret agent, in other words. At Golos's urging, Bentley embarked on a new odyssey, away from the CPUSA and into the Soviet underground secretly operating in the United States.

Elizabeth had much to learn from her new mentor. Golos spent months instructing her in the basic elements of spycraft: She learned how to notice when she was being followed by the police, how to elude capture, how to make secret phone calls, and how to handle clandestine correspondence.

"Underground methods were by now beginning to seem quite natural to me," she recalled. "I no longer thought it odd that I had to communicate with Timmy through a third party, that I must always use a pay phone when calling him, that if he could not come to my apartment we should always meet on out-of-the-way street corners. Whenever I had an appointment to see him, I was almost automatically on the alert to determine whether or not anyone was following me." Bentley also learned techniques for determining whether the FBI or police had gone through her belongings: "If I had to leave the apartment, I was careful to put [my belongings] in my black trunk and tie a thin black thread around it so that I would know if they had been tampered with in my absence."

As Bentley mastered the techniques of spying, her assignments for the Soviets grew. She spent the next two years as a courier, go-between, and manager of World Tourists, Inc., a travel business run by Golos that was actually a front operation for the Soviet Union. Together, they issued false passports and provided money and guidance to a growing network of Soviet informers and spies. As Golos's lover and his main espionage protégée, Elizabeth Bentley quickly became indispensable to Stalin's underground operation in the United States.

Communism's heyday in America lasted only a few years. In 1939, when the Soviet Union signed a nonaggression pact with Adolf Hitler, thousands of American party members resigned in disgust. But true believers like Elizabeth held on, ready to fight for the communist cause as the war clouds gathered.

When the United States entered World War II in 1941, its law-enforcement agencies began keeping an eye on all foreign agents operating inside America's borders, and the FBI soon caught Golos in one of its dragnets. He was tried, fined $500, and released. But he was exposed now and could no longer carry on his activities as a spymaster. So Golos and the NKVD turned to the person closest to him to take over his duties.

For the remainder of the war years, Elizabeth Bentley served as a spy handler and cashier for Soviet espionage operations in the United States—meeting with contacts in the government, creating fake passports for Russian agents, paying informants with Soviet money, and passing on information to the NKVD. Twice a month, Bentley took the train from New York to Washington to meet with Nathan and Helen Silvermaster, committed Communists who gathered secret US government documents from a large group of well-placed officials in Washington. Occasionally, Elizabeth would rendezvous with a Soviet agent in Washington by standing in front of a drugstore in Georgetown, wearing a red flower in her hat and holding a copy of *Life* magazine.

Elizabeth returned home on the train twice each month, her knitting bag stuffed with military documents, microfilm, and other secrets that she would pass along to Moscow.

Elizabeth's Soviet case officer was a Russian man

code-named JOHN. After her trips to Washington, they would meet secretly at newsreel theaters in Manhattan. "According to the plan," she said, "I was to enter the theater precisely on the hour, carrying a small attaché case containing any information to pass on, and sit down on the extreme right near the back. Ten minutes later he was to take the seat next to me, without any sign of recognition, and place an identical case on the floor next to mine. After a sufficient interval of time had elapsed, I was to pick up his briefcase and leave the theater."

Bentley was in deep, a Soviet agent operating quietly in the heart of the world's most powerful country. She knew that she was walking a tightrope, supporting a cause she believed in and a man she loved, all the while spying on the country she called home. Could this be treason? she wondered.

On a snowy Thanksgiving Day in 1943, after a large meal together at a local Manhattan restaurant, Bentley and Golos returned to her apartment, where he fell asleep on the couch—and never woke up. Jacob Golos was dead, of a heart attack.

Elizabeth's well-honed espionage skills kicked in immediately: She managed to conceal Jacob's true identity from the policemen who investigated his death, and she gathered and burned all his many papers in her apartment's fireplace. But she could not contain her desperation, her sense of being adrift once again. She drank heavily.

She quarreled with her new NKVD contacts at meetings and second-guessed their decisions.

The Soviets quickly caught on to the emotional distress and instability of their prized secret agent. With so much at stake, they had to step in.

Bit by bit, the NKVD began to take control over the different tentacles of Elizabeth's network, insisting that she hand over names and cease her usual espionage activities. When she objected, they flattered her—even going so far as to award her the Order of the Red Star in recognition of her service to the motherland.

Bentley began to question her loyalty to an organization and cause that no longer seemed to trust her. A trained spy, she watched her back at all times, sensing that she was being followed. Her suspicions gradually morphed into fear.

When the war ended, that fear turned to dread—and propelled Elizabeth Bentley into the hands of the FBI.

★ ★ ★

Elizabeth Bentley was the most well-connected Soviet spy ever to defect to the United States authorities. The information she handed over to the FBI included dozens of names of other Americans spying for the USSR, including people that the agency had been tracking for years. FBI agents dusted off old case files. Suddenly, old clues, in a new light, made sense.

"There wasn't any question in my mind that we hit gold on this one," one FBI agent commented.

FROM NEW YORK TO DIRECTOR AND SAC URGENT. RE
ELIZABETH TERRILL BENTLEY...ON NOVEMBER SEVENTH,
NINETEEN FORTY-FIVE THE ABOVE MENTIONED SUBJ.
VOLUNTARILY CAME TO THE NY FIELD DIVISION WHERE HSE
(SIC) FURNISHED INFORMATION RELATIVE TO A RUSSIAN
ESPIONAGE RING WITH WHICH SHE WAS AFFILIATED AND
WHICH IS PRESENTLY OPERATING IN THIS COUNTRY.

Text of cable sent from the FBI's New York office to
FBI director J. Edgar Hoover.

FBI director J. Edgar Hoover assigned seventy-two FBI agents to investigate the suspects Elizabeth had identified. Agents fanned out across the country, tailing unsuspecting government officials, listening in on private phone calls, opening mail, and photographing the men and women named in Elizabeth's confession. Three months after her jittery first approach to the FBI office in New Haven, Bentley had launched the biggest single case in the Bureau's history.

★ ★ ★

Hoover's FBI men stealthily scoured the nation for Soviet spies; the FBI director was not eager to risk tipping off his suspects by exposing Bentley as a defector. But he was not alone in his belief that the Soviets were engaged in foul play inside the United States. As the relationship between America and the Soviet Union soured overseas, more and more Americans tended to agree with him.

In February, a senior diplomat in the US embassy in Moscow named George Kennan sent a sobering message about the Soviet Union to his superiors in Washington. In what became known as the "Long Telegram," Kennan argued that Soviet leadership had no choice but to paint the United States as their sworn nemesis, because it needed an external enemy to justify the Communist Party's rigid control over its society. The USSR could not be trusted or negotiated with. Likening communism to a disease, Kennan contended that it would respond only to force, or what he called "containment." The Long Telegram was copied, talked about, and passed all over Washington. Its conclusions soon leaked out to the general public.

Barely two weeks later, on March 5, the former British prime minister Winston Churchill delivered a speech in Fulton, Missouri—with President Truman seated in the audience—that conjured an image of an "iron curtain" separating the communist and noncommunist countries. Like Truman, Churchill feared that the Soviets were establishing a zone of total control over Central Europe. "Behind that line," he intoned, "lie all the capitals of the ancient states of Central and Eastern Europe...all these famous cities and the populations around them lie in what I must call the Soviet sphere, and all are subject, in one form or another, not only to Soviet influence but to a very high and in many cases increasing measure of control from Moscow."

Stalin called Churchill's speech "an appeal to war with the USSR."

By the summer of 1946, Americans everywhere started seeing signs of communist traitors in their midst. Newspapers took an increasingly dark view of the USSR's motives. The Republican Party, eager to score points against President Truman, a Democrat, accused him of being "soft on communism" and willing to turn a blind eye to subversives in his own administration.

Truman tried to mollify his critics by instituting a new loyalty program for the federal government. All two million federal employees would be screened individually for "membership in, affiliation with or sympathetic association with any foreign or domestic organization, association, movement, group or combination of persons designated by the Attorney General as totalitarian, fascist, communist or subversive." Attorney General Tom C. Clark developed a list of these organizations, which included everything from African American civil rights groups to labor unions and virtually anyone associated with communism or the Soviet Union.

Clark's list took on a life of its own. Schools, local

governments, and private companies used it to fire, expel, or exclude anyone considered disloyal to the United States. An accusation was enough to ruin a person's reputation; in the shadow of a looming Soviet menace, many Americans jettisoned the most basic standards of due process, fairness, or the presumption of innocence.

Truman's program quickly snowballed into a general hunt for internal enemies, a "red scare" that gradually infected the imaginations of millions of American citizens.

Later that year, in the fall of 1947, a previously obscure committee of the US House of Representatives took the hunt to a new level. The House Un-American Activities Committee (or HUAC) announced that it would begin investigating the influence of the Communist Party on Hollywood and the movie business. The committee sent subpoenas to dozens of well-known actors, directors, screenwriters, and other professionals suspected of being affiliated with communism.

HUAC pressed each one of them with what became known as the "sixty-four-thousand-dollar question": "Are you now, or have you ever been, a member of the Communist Party of the United States?"

Some of the accused named names, fingering friends and colleagues in the entertainment industry. Others denied having any ties to the Soviets. But a small group known as the Hollywood Ten refused to answer questions, citing the First Amendment of the US Constitution, which grants citizens the freedom of speech and association. In the fall of 1947, that was a losing argument. The ten directors and screenwriters were thrown in prison for contempt of Congress. Americans sent them hate mail. Following their release, they were "blacklisted," prevented from working in Hollywood ever again.

HUAC's hearings riveted the nation—and ratcheted up J. Edgar Hoover's frustration with the FBI's increasingly fruitless investigation into Elizabeth Bentley's allegations. Bentley's confessions convinced him that the United States had been infiltrated by Soviet spies. But wherever Hoover's vaunted G-men (for "government men") looked, the trail went cold. Doors were locked; promising leads ended up as dead ends. It was almost as if the Soviets had been tipped off to the fact that the FBI was on to them.

But that was impossible, Hoover thought. Other than a few FBI officials, Hoover had only shared this intelligence with America's closest ally, Great Britain.

No one in the US government was better informed about Soviet activities in the United States than J. Edgar Hoover. But not even Hoover had any inkling about the mole—or secret Soviet agent—hiding in the top ranks of Great Britain's spy agency, MI6.

In 1945, the head of Soviet counterintelligence for MI6 was Kim Philby, a respected agent who many believed would someday rise to be Britain's spy chief. Philby had a dark secret. In the 1930s, the Soviets secretly recruited him and a group of fellow students at Cambridge University. The "Cambridge Spy Ring"—which included Philby, Donald Maclean, Guy Burgess, Anthony Blunt, and John Cairncross—made sure that almost nothing that England or its allies did would be kept secret from the USSR. Inside the NKVD, the group was referred to as "the Magnificent Five."

Thanks to Philby, word of Bentley's defection ricocheted back to the highest levels of the Soviet government, which ordered its agents in the United States to "cease immediately their connection with all persons known to Bentley in our work [and] to warn the agents about Bentley's betrayal."

"Because of the successful delivery of that message," wrote one historian, "the FBI's massive undercover effort over the next eighteen months would be in vain. Thanks to Philby, Elizabeth would become the least successful double agent in FBI history."

★ ★ ★

By the summer of 1948, J. Edgar Hoover was ready to try a new tactic against his Soviet adversary. If he couldn't track down Russian spies and bring them to trial, perhaps he could flush them out into the open.

Against the law, Hoover began passing classified files to his contacts on HUAC, with documents describing

Bentley's alleged spy ring. The opportunity to go public with a genuine communist conspiracy was too good for the Republican congressmen of HUAC to pass up. In July of that year, the committee announced a new round of investigations, but this time into something far more serious than the communist infiltration of Hollywood.

HUAC was going to investigate the Soviet spy networks operating inside the US government itself. On August 1, 1948, the woman now dubbed the "Red Spy Queen" was their first witness.

For two days, in a congressional hearing room packed with spectators and news reporters, as flashbulbs went off and news cameras whirred, Elizabeth Bentley revealed the sensational details of her spying for the Soviet Union. Bentley told all: She named names, exposed her Russian contacts, and painted a shocking picture of a vast communist conspiracy operating in the United States.

MR. RANKIN: But he was in the employ of the federal government?

MISS BENTLEY: That is correct; yes.

MR. RANKIN: He was a member of the Communist Party, you say?

MISS BENTLEY: That is correct.

MR. RANKIN: And an agent of the Communist International?

MISS BENTLEY: Probably an agent of the NKVD would be more correct.

MR. RANKIN: That is the Russian Communist secret police?

MISS BENTLEY: That is correct.

MR. RANKIN: And the Communists are dedicated to the overthrow of this government; is that right?

MISS BENTLEY: That is right.

An excerpt of Elizabeth Bentley's testimony before HUAC, in which she answers questions about Nathan Silvermaster, her main contact in Washington, DC, from Congressman John E. Rankin of Mississippi.

On July 2, headlines all over the United States announced the exploits of the "lady spy," "Comrade Woman," "nutmeg Mata Hari," and the "blonde and blue-eyed" (Bentley was neither) defector. That Bentley was native born, from an old Massachusetts family, and educated at one of America's top colleges made her seem more threatening; anybody, it seemed, could succumb to the lure of the communist menace.

The very next day, another defector appeared before HUAC, whose shocking testimony added heft to the Red Spy Queen's claims. Like Bentley, Whittaker Chambers— a prominent journalist for *Time* magazine—spent years as an underground Soviet agent in the 1930s, cultivating informers and passing secret documents to his contacts in the GRU, the USSR's military intelligence service. But unlike Bentley, Chambers had been disgusted by Stalin's willingness to make a pact with Hitler in 1939. He escaped from his Soviet handlers, always fearful that he might end up dead by an assassin's bullet. In the 1940s, he rejected communism and rediscovered his religious beliefs.

Chambers made a stunning accusation that day: He charged a man named Alger Hiss, one of Washington's most respected government officials, with spying for the Soviet Union. And Chambers admitted that he himself had been Hiss's "handler" for the NKVD.

Alger Hiss was the president of the Carnegie Endowment for International Peace in Washington, the nation's most prestigious research institute. During the Depression, he had served as an official in the New Deal's Agricultural Adjustment Administration, and he later moved on to a senior post at the US State Department. In 1945, Hiss had led the group of international diplomats who eventually signed the United Nations Charter. He had many important and respected friends, and even President Truman expressed disbelief at the allegations.

On August 5, Hiss appeared before HUAC and testified that he had never been a Communist, nor had he ever met Whittaker Chambers. The stage was set for the first and most sensational face-off of the Cold War era in the United States. "Hiss versus Chambers" divided politicians, reporters, and millions of average citizens into two camps: those who believed that Hiss was a spy and those who argued that HUAC's methods had descended into a "witch hunt" that sought to destroy an innocent, patriotic public servant.

When Chambers made the same allegations over the radio, Alger Hiss sued him for slander.

Chambers had already produced a pile of incriminating documents. He now led HUAC investigators to his farm in Maryland, where he produced several rolls of microfilm that he had hidden inside a hollowed-out pumpkin. He claimed that Hiss had passed these to him several years earlier, as part of their conspiracy to provide information to the Soviet Union. The "Pumpkin Papers" emerged as Exhibit A in Alger Hiss's prosecution, in a trial that lasted from November 1949 to January 1950.

President Truman called the trial a "red herring," and Secretary of State Dean Acheson declared, "I do not intend to turn my back on Alger Hiss." But on January 21, Hiss was convicted of perjury relating to his alleged espionage; he could not be tried as a spy because the five-year statute of limitations had run out. The judge sentenced Alger Hiss to five years in prison.

The first spy to be trapped in the Cold War's net maintained his innocence until his death.

★ ★ ★

Fears of communism had smoldered for much of the decade; Elizabeth Bentley's testimony was the fuel that this fire needed to explode. A single spy-defector had opened Americans' eyes to the new threat to their way of life. Egged on by HUAC, Americans now sensed that the Soviet Union might have agents anywhere—even in the US government itself. And the truth was that the NKVD operated inside the United States with near impunity throughout the 1930s and '40s. The FBI was learning, but it still had only the faintest idea of the enemy it faced on American soil.

The USSR now controlled the field of battle, but not for long. It would take a different kind of soldier, and new technologies, to bring the fight to the Soviets.

FBI agent Robert Lamphere in the 1940s, when he was the Bureau's top spy hunter.

Corbis/Bettmann Archive

2

THE SPY HUNTERS

FBI agent Robert Lamphere had heard about the contents of the safe in his boss's office. Rumors spread that the Army Security Agency had cracked a Soviet communication code, yet for some reason his boss kept the ASA documents locked away. Curiosity gnawed at him. "Every counterintelligence man's dream is to be able to secretly read the enemy's communications," Lamphere reflected.

Lamphere guessed that the information inside his

boss's safe held the key to something big, something that might finally give him the upper hand in his years-long hunt for Soviet spies in America.

Elizabeth Bentley's revelations had tipped off the Soviet spies themselves—ironically making them harder to catch. "We were near and yet so far," Lamphere recalled. "Bentley had shown that Russians were operating all around us, but we were unable to counter their efforts.

"We felt hamstrung," Lamphere said, "facing an enemy that did not fight by the rules of decency or fairness; we believed the FBI had to become more aggressive in counterintelligence against the Soviets or we would lose the war against the KGB."

Lamphere joined the FBI in 1941, at the age of twenty-three. He had grown up in Idaho during the Great Depression, working summers as a miner to pay for college, and was eager to jump into the ranks of the G-men.

His first assignment in the New York City field office gave him the adventure he was looking for. He learned his trade swiftly. It didn't hurt that he looked the part. One writer provided a vivid description of Lamphere: "square-jawed, broad-shouldered, thick black hair with a precise part, and, not least, deep brown eyes that would hold a person with a gaze as steady as a marksman's."

When the Bureau promoted him in 1944 to the Soviet Espionage Division, in Washington, DC, Lamphere despaired at first. "I liked criminal cases.... You could do a good job and have a sense of completion," he said. But "the enemy just went on and on; when you got rid of one spy, another would take his place. How would you get satisfaction?"

Lamphere could not have guessed how much the world would change in just a few short years—or that the Soviet Espionage Division would quickly become the center of the action for the FBI.

★ ★ ★

"I'd like to take charge of the messages the ASA sent over," Lamphere announced to his boss.

To Lamphere's surprise, his boss agreed.

With that, Lamphere's FBI career would veer off in a new and unpredictable direction. "The KGB messages were to change my life," he recalled. First, though, he had to meet his new partner.

The hub of code breaking in the United States was a tiny office in Arlington Hall, formerly a private school for girls in Virginia, not far from Washington, DC. Employing just nineteen people, the US Army's Signal Intelligence Service interpreted secret messages captured from Nazi Germany, Imperial Japan, and the Soviet Union. (Later, in the 1950s, the service would become the National Security Agency, or NSA, a huge government organization charged with secretly monitoring communications all over the world.)

In the early 1940s, the United States managed to intercept a mountain of cable telegram traffic from Soviet embassies. Soviet cable operators tapped out messages on special devices, and these messages traveled via underground (and underwater) cable in the form of specially coded signals.

The Soviets took extra precautions to keep their communications secret. Their code clerks were carefully trained and followed strict procedures set by Moscow.

First, a Russian-language message was encrypted using a codebook shared among the different embassies and government offices. The codebook was like a dictionary, enabling the code clerk to translate a message into a secret language, comprehensible only to those with access to it. Using these codebooks as a guide, message clerks converted text into four-digit numerical sequences.

Encoding provided a measure of security but was not fail-safe. In 1941, for example, Finnish soldiers overran a Soviet consulate in Petsamo, Finland, and after a fierce gun battle managed to capture a partially burned codebook. The book was later confiscated by the German army, and it was eventually found in the basement of a castle in Germany by American soldiers in 1945, just before the Nazi surrender.

As insurance against such accidents, the Soviet clerks then wrapped their messages in an additional layer of secrecy, using what were known as "one-time pads." A one-time pad contained randomly generated sets of numbers, organized in groups of five, that were added mathematically to the encoded, numbered messages.

Only two copies of the one-time pads existed: one held by the sender, and the other by the recipient of the message. Immediately after using a page of the one-time pad, both the sender and the recipient would destroy it.

And yet... through painstaking work, day after day, the cryptographers at Arlington Hall began to pick up fragmented meanings in the Soviet cables. Patterns began to emerge. Code names of secret agents took shape.

It turned out that the Soviet one-time pad system had a weakness.

In 1941, Hitler's armies invaded Russia and advanced toward Moscow, wreaking havoc in the Soviets' communications networks. More and more secret communications demanded more one-time pads—and at some point in 1942 or 1943, Soviet cryptographers started making multiple copies of the same pads, to save time.

In the middle of a war for survival, given the sheer volume of messages traded back and forth among Soviet embassies and the government in Moscow, making multiple copies must have seemed an insignificant decision. How could they have imagined that a silent, determined team of Americans, thousands of miles away in the peaceful countryside near Washington, might pick up on this simple error?

Using an early IBM computer to pore through patterns in 10,000 Soviet cables, Arlington Hall cryptanalysts found seven duplicated ciphers—seven instances in which a Soviet code clerk must have used a one-time pad more than once. Soon they found more—and then more. In time, the Americans managed to "strip" the cipher completely from a group of Soviet cables.

All that was left was to unlock the remaining layer of encryption. And, as it turned out, the Soviet codebook first captured in Finland finally found its way to the United States—to the desk of Meredith Gardner.

In the secret world of cryptanalysis, Meredith Gardner had earned a reputation as something of an oddball superstar. He joined the Signal Intelligence Service early in the war and mastered the Japanese language in three months in order to join the fight to crack Japan's secret military communications. He went on to learn Russian. Gardner possessed a keen, logical mind as well as—by his own description—"a sort of magpie attitude to facts, the habit of storing things away that did not seem to have any connection at all."

Gardner realized immediately that the battered, burned volume was an old codebook. On its own, it would not serve as the dictionary he needed, but it was filled with cues and gave him an incomplete road map to the minds of the Soviet cryptographers.

In 1947, Gardner had compiled all of his initial research

into a secret memo titled "Special Analysis Report No. 1." He described cover names, fragmentary messages, traces of the work of Soviet agents operating deep under cover in the United States. His report made it to the desk of the head of the FBI's Counterespionage Section—but, lacking specifics that could spark an investigation, the official locked the report in an old safe in his office. And that's where Bob Lamphere eventually found it.

"From the first I was curious as to how Gardner had gotten even as far as he had in breaking into the KGB code system," Lamphere said. "Little by little, I came to understand what had happened."

By 1947, when Robert Lamphere first entered the gates of Arlington Hall, Gardner had been working doggedly to reconstruct the Russian codebook for nearly two years. He was getting close.

The top secret project—which would not be revealed to the public for fifty years—was code-named VENONA.

Even the street-smart and experienced Lamphere was not prepared for Gardner's personality or his unusual brilliance. Gardner was tall, lanky, quiet, and intense. He toiled silently at a desk inside the Russian Section, which, like all departments, was locked, heavily guarded, and subject to strict rules about what could be taken in—or out.

"You'll find Meredith Gardner a shy, introverted loner," Gardner's boss told Lamphere, adding, "you'll have a hard time getting to know him." That wasn't an exaggeration. Lamphere's first meeting with Gardner was not promising.

"I told him I was intensely interested in what he was doing and would be willing to mount any sort of research effort to provide him with more information," Lamphere recalled. Gardner "simply nodded." But the stubborn FBI agent did not discourage so easily. Several weeks passed, with Lamphere returning to Gardner's desk periodically to ask the same question: What could he do to help?

Finally, after a long pause, Gardner asked Lamphere whether it might be possible to get his hands on "plaintext" cables (or the text of messages before they had been encoded or enciphered) from Soviet officials in 1944—so that he might be able to compare them to the pages of code he was struggling to unlock.

Lamphere agreed, though the request was akin to asking, "How about the key to the vault at Fort Knox?"

Still, it finally seemed as if the two men might be able to work together. Gardner's world was the abstract realm of codes, clues, and interpretation. What he lacked was the real-world information that could fill in the gaps of the puzzle he was assembling.

And that was precisely where Lamphere's FBI savvy came in. Lamphere and his FBI colleagues turned up a thick package of plaintext Soviet cables—most likely stolen, he guessed, during a wartime "black bag" operation (a search that had taken place without a warrant). The cables were exactly what Gardner had been dreaming of.

Lamphere delivered the cables to his new partner. Two weeks later, he returned to Arlington Hall, where he found Gardner "in the most excited mood I'd ever seen him display."

★ ★ ★

The FBI agent and the cryptanalyst knew they were on to something important. But neither man grasped how crucial their research would be to the outcome of the conflict smoldering halfway across the globe.

A world away from Lamphere and Gardner's quiet deliberations in Arlington Hall, American and Soviet forces in Europe inched toward open hostility. Stalin's Red Army and his NKVD units had tightened their hold on Eastern Europe, clamping down on dissent and refusing free elections where they would challenge his control. For the Soviet leader, the issue was crystal clear: Russia must protect its security at all costs. America and its Western allies, in contrast, saw Stalin's intransigence as the actions of a new Hitler, someone bent on undoing all they had fought and died for.

These two worldviews collided head-on on June 24, 1948, when the Soviet military cut off all roads and rail routes to the Western sector of Berlin, the area controlled by the United States, France, and Great Britain. The next day, the USSR abruptly cut off food shipments and electricity.

Stalin, who had hoped to occupy all of Berlin, assumed that the Allies would simply back down; after all, barely 25,000 American, French, and German soldiers remained in the city, which was now surrounded by 1.5 million Soviet troops. Moreover, the city's Western sector had only a month's worth of food and fuel supplies. It would be just a matter of time, the Soviets reasoned, before the Americans would be forced to abandon the city.

But the Soviet leader had gravely miscalculated. The American commander, General Lucius Clay, gave the US response: "We are convinced that our remaining in Berlin is essential to our prestige in Germany and in Europe. Whether for good or bad, it has become a symbol of the American intent." Clay's announcement reflected simple geography: West Berlin floated like a tiny island in the sea of eastern Germany, a region completely controlled by the Soviets. If the United States backed down here, in Hitler's former capital, who would trust it to stand up to Stalin anywhere else?

President Truman decided to call Stalin's bluff. The United States defied the blockade with a massive airlift of supply planes that flew over Soviet forces and directly into Tempelhof Airport in the Western sector of Berlin. Truman also delivered a sterner warning to Stalin: The president sent a fleet of B-29 bombers to bases in England, the same type of aircraft that had dropped atomic bombs on Hiroshima and Nagasaki. The fleet was not, in fact, outfitted with nuclear weapons, but the message was clear. Truman would order an atomic attack "if it became necessary."

The allies dispatched more than 200,000 flights to Berlin over the next year, wearing down Stalin's resolve and sending a powerful message of hope, not only to the besieged residents of the city but to all of Europe. In May 1949, Stalin capitulated, and the Soviet Union suspended its blockade.

America's nuclear gambit had kept Stalin in check, but the crisis in Berlin underscored the need to anticipate the USSR's next move. To meet this challenge, America's intelligence agencies had few resources and only a handful of agents at their disposal. The newly formed Central Intelligence Agency, not yet two years old, was a fledgling organization with a motley staff. In the late 1940s, the United States had no spies in the Soviet Union. The handful of spies in Berlin were the closest to America's communist adversary—and none of them spoke Russian. In the summer of 1949, the only American agents capable of uncovering the USSR's true motives were hunkered down in a closely guarded office in Arlington Hall.

★ ★ ★

On September 1, 1949, Stalin taught America a hard lesson about the cost of lagging behind in the spy wars. On that day, US reconnaissance aircraft flying from bases in Japan and outfitted with special detection equipment picked up signs of nuclear debris in the atmosphere. Within days, American scientists determined that the USSR had detonated its own nuclear bomb in the eastern Soviet republic of Kazakhstan. The Americans dubbed the weapon, roughly the size of the American bombs dropped on Nagasaki, "Joe-1," after Joseph Stalin.

Americans learned of the Soviet atomic test three weeks after it occurred, and President Truman did his best to calmly reveal to the media that the United States' main adversary had acquired the most destructive weapon in history. The next day, newspaper headlines howled, RUSSIA HAS ATOMIC BOMB and TRUMAN SAYS REDS HAVE EXPLODED ATOM.

The news of the Soviet nuclear test set off a panic inside the American government. US officials had known that the Soviets would eventually be able to build a nuclear weapon, but the nation's top intelligence experts estimated that the Soviets' nuclear capability was still four years away. America's spies had simply missed the evidence of Stalin's progress. The United States' brief monopoly on the world's most powerful weapon came to a sudden, shocking end.

It didn't take long for the implications to sink in: Ever

since World War II, the bomb had given the United States a significant military advantage over the Soviet Union, even though the Red Army had many more soldiers and armaments in Eastern Europe. Now that calculus had changed overnight.

Russia *already* possessed long-range bombers able to fly thousands of miles—enough to reach the US mainland. Stuart Symington, the secretary of the Air Force, articulated Americans' fears in their starkest terms. "Should Russia use the relatively simple and completely proven process of refueling in flight," he observed, "she would now have the capacity to deliver the bomb" into the American homeland. How should America respond to this new reality?

For President Truman and his national security advisers, the situation demanded only one answer: to build more and bigger atomic bombs. Truman accelerated the development of the "superbomb," or hydrogen bomb, a weapon that would be one thousand times as powerful as the bomb dropped on Hiroshima. A new kind of competition between Russia and the United States took shape that fall, a nuclear arms race that quickly raised the stakes of the Cold War to unforeseen and terrifying heights.

★ ★ ★

The Soviets' first nuclear test presented a vexing question for Agent Robert Lamphere. "Had they been aided in their effort to build [the bomb]," he wondered, "by information stolen from the United States?" If so, then the culprits were still at large—and still able to steal American nuclear secrets and pass them on to the Russians. VENONA was no longer solely about exposing Stalin's spy networks; it was about stealing the USSR's advantage in the new nuclear arms race.

VENONA had given Lamphere clues, but not answers. "I stood in the vestibule of the enemy's house, having entered by stealth," Lamphere recalled. "I held in my hand a set of keys. Each would fit one of the doors of the place and lead us, I hoped, to matters of importance to our country. I had no idea where the corridors in the KGB edifice would take us, or what we would find when we reached the end of a search—but the keys were ours, and we were determined to use them."

The most tantalizing bit of information to have emerged from Meredith Gardner's VENONA decryptions was a Soviet cable from 1944 that included fragmentary information about a scientific paper from inside the Manhattan Project, the top secret US program that designed and built the atomic bomb. The message read:

...received from Rest (code name) the third part of Report "SN-12 Efferent Fluctuations in a Steam Diffusion Method"-work his specialty.

Lamphere had to rely on old-fashioned detective work to probe the significance of this message. He managed to track down a copy of the actual scientific paper and to persuade scientists at the US Atomic Energy Commission to explain to him what it meant. What he learned shocked him. The "report" mentioned in this decrypted message described a crucial step in building an atomic bomb. "It became immediately obvious to me," Lamphere said, "that the Russians had indeed stolen crucial research from us and had undoubtedly used it to build their bomb." The front page of the paper included its author's name, K. Fuchs.

Lamphere scrambled to find out everything he could about K. Fuchs. But as his investigation grew, more names—and equally likely suspects—appeared on the FBI agent's radar. The hunt was accelerating; Lamphere recruited more fellow FBI agents to help track down his spy.

K. Fuchs, Lamphere learned, was Klaus Fuchs, a German-born British physicist who joined the Manhattan Project with a team from Great Britain. As with the agent code-named REST, the diffusion method was Fuchs's area of expertise. Could REST be Fuchs himself—Stalin's agent inside America's secret nuclear weapons lab? He could not be certain, and with so much at stake, Lamphere knew he had to dig deeper. If REST was Fuchs, what was his motive for spying?

Lamphere's team soon turned up a document from

the Gestapo—the Nazi secret police—that had been cap-
tured during the war and had fallen into the hands of the
FBI. The document revealed that in the early 1930s, the
Gestapo had ordered the arrest of a young scientist named
Klaus Fuchs because he was a member of the Communist
Party. Fuchs had escaped to England one step ahead of
Hitler's agents in the 1930s. That got Lamphere's attention.
Additional VENONA messages deciphered by Meredith
Gardner revealed further details about REST: that he had
worked at Los Alamos, the main research center for the
Manhattan Project; that he had a sister; and that he had
traveled to Chicago in 1945. All three clues fit Klaus Fuchs
perfectly.

"I became convinced that Klaus Fuchs was the prime
suspect," Lamphere said.

By then, Fuchs had returned home to England, and
Lamphere reached out to his counterparts in MI5, the British equivalent of the FBI, to track him down. Skilled interrogators from MI5 invited Fuchs to meetings over several
weeks, gradually eliciting different details of his involvement in the Soviets' espionage ring. On January 24, 1950,
Klaus Fuchs broke down and confessed.

In March, a British court convicted Fuchs of espionage
and sentenced him to fourteen years in prison. (He was
released after nine years, and on leaving prison immediately moved to communist East Germany.)

The capture and confession of Klaus Fuchs were like

a dam breaking in Lamphere's and Gardner's years-long accumulation of clues, leads, and evidence of an active Soviet espionage ring in the United States. The KGB agent in charge of the ring, Alexander Feklisov, later recalled his foreboding sense that his spy network was about to be "rolled up": "When dominoes are lined up," he said, "the first one to fall draws all the others with it."

In a cascade of discoveries, their work led them to Fuchs's courier, Harry Gold; then to David Greenglass, a Manhattan Project employee; then to David's sister, Ethel; and finally to Ethel's husband—a man named Julius Rosenberg. In her confession to the FBI five years earlier, Elizabeth Bentley recalled that Jacob Golos had introduced her to a man named Julius, who passed information on to the Soviets.

In the end, Julius Rosenberg, code-named LIBERAL in the VENONA cables, emerged from the shadows as the accused ringleader of a large, active network of Soviet spies in the United States, a network that had betrayed America's nuclear secrets. Arrests, indictments, and a torrent of media coverage flooded the case of the atomic spies. From their arrests in 1950 through their 1951 trial in New York City to their eventual execution by electric chair in 1953, the Rosenbergs made front-page news.

The Rosenberg case also helped inspire a little-known senator from Wisconsin, named Joseph McCarthy, to give an inflammatory speech in Wheeling, West Virginia, on

February 9, 1950, in which he claimed (without evidence) that "I have here in my hand…a list of names that were made known to the Secretary of State as being members of the Communist Party and who nevertheless are still working and shaping policy in the State Department." The news media latched onto McCarthy's speech and catapulted him to national prominence as the most aggressive anticommunist leader in the United States. "McCarthyism" became a catchphrase for the hunt for communist subversives, a frenzy that would engulf the United States for the rest of the 1950s.

Robert Lamphere and Meredith Gardner witnessed the unfolding Rosenberg trial through a different lens, one that only a handful of Americans could appreciate. They knew that the cracking of the VENONA codes was a secret victory over the NKVD. Thanks to the persistence of this unlikely duo, Stalin's spies were finally being pushed out of the United States.

But with both superpowers now holding nuclear weapons, the stakes had gotten much higher and the battlefield even larger. Already the Soviets maneuvered for control of Europe, where their espionage networks held the advantage over America and its Western allies. In this new and unpredictable world, the CIA could only scramble to keep up. And, as if on cue, the next big battle of the Cold War caught America off guard, half a world away.

The spy George Blake, during his years working for MI6, in the 1940s.

3

THE DOUBLE

On Sunday, June 25, 1950, the spy George Blake sat in a church service in Seoul, the capital of South Korea. Somebody was whispering behind him.

Blake was not a particularly religious man, though going to church did make him nostalgic for his Protestant upbringing in Holland before World War II. Now, however, his interest in religion was mostly strategic. As Great Britain's top agent in Korea, Blake made it his business to hobnob with the South Korean elite—its politicians, businessmen, and generals—many of whom were Korean Christians who had lived in the United States before and during the war.

All of Korea had been ruled by Imperial Japan since 1910. During this time, under the increasingly harsh conditions of Japanese occupation, two movements for Korean independence took root: one led by Communists and supported by the Soviets, and the other a pro-American movement led by Syngman Rhee. After Japan's defeat in 1945, control of the Korean Peninsula split down the middle, at the 38th parallel, a line that cut the nation neatly in half. North of the line, forces of the Soviet Red Army moved in and eventually established a Communist government led by Kim Il-Sung. In the south, with the help of the American military, Syngman Rhee became president of Western-allied South Korea in 1948.

Most Soviet and American soldiers went home after 1948, and many assumed that Korea would eventually unify under a single government.

Instead, the two sides skirmished along the border, as Syngman Rhee and Kim Il-Sung traded insults and accusations of aggression. And immediately beyond Korea's borders, Chinese Communists led by Mao Zedong seized control of the mainland in 1949, following a four-year-long civil war with the nationalist forces of Chiang Kai-shek. Mao offered moral support and—more important—the promise of military backing to his North Korean neighbors. The stage was set, it seemed, for a new conflagration in East Asia.

Blake turned around and saw an American officer, spreading word quietly to the other American military men in the church sanctuary. "One by one they tiptoed out, leaving their wives behind," he remarked.

Clearly something unusual had happened, Blake thought.

After the service, as the remaining worshippers gathered outside the church, news whipsawed through the crowd that North Korean troops had crossed the 38th parallel. Over the next two days, North Korean soldiers charged past the dividing line, scattering South Korea's military forces. On June 27, Syngman Rhee, along with the entire South Korean leadership, abandoned Seoul, leaving its citizens unguarded.

President Truman, who had wanted to avoid getting bogged down in Korea, now faced the prospect of another major country falling to the Communists. "I felt certain," he said, "that if South Korea was allowed to fall, Communist leaders would be emboldened to override nations closer to our own shores. If the Communists were permitted to force their way into the Republic of Korea without opposition from the free world, no small nation would have the courage to resist threat and aggression by stronger Communist neighbors."

Thousands of US troops were already stationed at

American bases in occupied Japan, just a short hop across the Sea of Japan from Korea. Within weeks, they began streaming onto the Korean Peninsula, shoring up the battered remnants of the South Korean forces and joining the battle against North Korea. Almost out of nowhere, the Korean War had begun. Armed conflict between communism and democracy was no longer a frightening possibility but a terrifying reality.

★ ★ ★

George Blake's family spanned continents and political beliefs. He was born in Rotterdam, Holland, in 1922; his father was an Egyptian Jew, and his mother a Dutch Protestant. George had a close relationship with an Egyptian cousin, Henri Curiel, a leading Communist organizer who later moved to France and was assassinated in 1978, most likely for his political activities. Henri once took George on a visit to his father's (George's uncle's) estate in Al Mansouria, in the Nile delta, to demonstrate the wretched conditions under which peasants lived. Before long, Henri's beliefs led him to found the Communist Party of Egypt. His young cousin admired Henri's passion for action and rejection of inequality. But at this point in his life, communism held no appeal for George, who considered himself a devout Christian. Communism was the declared enemy of God, George recalled thinking. "This alone was enough for me to condemn it utterly and doom it forever," he reflected.

In May of 1940, when George was only seventeen, he was swept up into World War II. That spring, he witnessed Germany's tanks rumbling into his hometown as its air force, the Luftwaffe, pounded the city from above. The Dutch military held out for barely three weeks before surrendering to Hitler.

At that young age, George joined the Dutch underground resistance movement as a courier, learning to dodge the Gestapo, the Nazi secret police. Evading arrest, he eventually escaped to England, where he enlisted in the Royal Navy to fight against Germany.

George's stint in the Royal Navy didn't last long: His reputation for personal bravery in the Dutch underground and his cosmopolitan family tree attracted the attention of Britain's Secret Intelligence Service (SIS), also known as MI6. MI6 invited George to join its espionage campaign against the Nazis. He accepted immediately. Blake underwent additional training and was on his way to becoming a spy for his adopted home.

When the war ended, George was an MI6 officer whose star was on the rise. Two years later, when Blake was only twenty-five years old, MI6 sent him to Korea, on a mission to establish a new network of spies in the Far East.

★ ★ ★

"The first day of the [Korean] war was one of confusion and conflicting reports. Nobody seemed to know exactly what was happening," Blake recalled. "We spent that night burning our codes and secret documents in a sheltered corner of the garden in the hope that the bonfire would not attract the attention of the North Korean military."

Within days, the North Koreans discovered Blake and took him prisoner along with a group of British diplomats and civilians. The terrified captives were driven out of the city in a truck; George was certain that they were all about to be executed. "After all we had heard about the Communists," he said, "this seemed to us the only explanation which fitted the circumstances."

Instead, the truck continued on to Pyongyang, the North Korean capital, passing through a hellish landscape of burned-out villages and rotting corpses along the way. In Pyongyang, the weary prisoners were confined with several hundred others in an abandoned school building, where they remained for nearly two months. This ragged group then joined several hundred American prisoners of war on a forced trek to Mampo, a small town on the Yalu River, which forms the border between North Korea and China. "There we were put up in derelict army huts," he recalled, "but our living conditions were reasonable."

On September 15, 1950, that brief period of calm was suddenly shattered when General Douglas A. MacArthur, a hero of the Pacific theater of World War II, formulated a brilliant surprise attack at Incheon, a peninsula just south of Seoul. Following a skillful amphibious landing, more than 75,000 American and South Korean troops punched forward against the North Korean army.

Two weeks later, they retook Seoul.

MacArthur then pushed his luck, sending his army across the 38th parallel and racing toward the Yalu River. On October 15, MacArthur—ignoring intelligence reports that he was stretching his army too thin and risked provoking the Chinese military—told President Truman that the war would be over soon and the troops would be home by Christmas.

At that very moment, more than a quarter million Chinese soldiers massed on the Chinese side of the Yalu, preparing a surprise attack in support of their Communist neighbor.

What followed was one of the biggest disasters in all of American military history. The Chinese shattered MacArthur's armies, causing thousands of casualties and forcing the Americans back beyond the 38th parallel in barely more than two weeks. In early January 1952, the Communists once again captured Seoul. In retaliation, MacArthur ordered massive bombing strikes against "every installation, factory, city, and village" in North Korea. A *New York Times* reporter described the outcome for one small village:

The inhabitants throughout the village and in the fields were caught and killed and kept the exact postures they held when the napalm struck–a man about to get on his bicycle, fifty boys and girls playing in an orphanage, a housewife strangely unmarked, holding in her hand a page torn from a Sears-Roebuck catalogue crayoned at Mail Order No. 3,811,294 for a $2.98 "bewitching bed jacket–coral."

For George Blake and his fellow prisoners, now being moved from location to location by their captors, all of North Korea had become a scorched war zone. "We walked all day through wild mountain country," he recounted, "stopping at night in deserted villages where we sometimes found only burnt-out shells instead of houses.

"Sometimes our column was attacked by American fighters," he recalled, "which, sweeping down low, machine-gunned us so that we had to scatter hastily in ditches and fields. People who couldn't keep up and fell behind were shot by the Korean guards."

During these dark days and terrifying nights, Blake's opinions about the war—and about which side was right, and which was wrong—began to change. "I remembered how in Holland, during the war," Blake said, "when I heard at night the drone of heavy RAF planes overhead on their way to bomb Germany, the sound had been like a song to me."

Now, seeing firsthand "the enormous grey hulks of the American bombers sweeping low to drop their deadly load over the small, defenseless Korean villages huddled against the mountainside, when I saw the villagers, mostly women and children and old people—for the men were all at the front—being machine-gunned as they fled to seek shelter in the fields, I felt nothing but shame and anger."

In April 1952, President Truman fired MacArthur after the general made public statements disagreeing with the president over how the war should be waged. (One of these differences may have been over whether or not to use nuclear weapons against North Korea and China; in an interview two years later, the general boasted, "I could have won the war in Korea in a maximum of ten days....I would have dropped between thirty and fifty atomic bombs on [Communist China's] air bases and other depots strung across the neck of Manchuria.") MacArthur believed that China could be defeated; Truman and his advisers were convinced that a wider war with China would trigger a global conflict and draw in the Soviet Union.

MacArthur's replacement, General Matthew Ridgway, managed to turn the tide against the enemy, with both sides settling once again along the 38th parallel. Ridgway had saved South Korea but did not end the war. It took two more years before the two sides signed a truce.

★ ★ ★

For most of those two years, Blake and a small group of prisoners languished in a makeshift North Korean prison camp, plagued with monotony and boredom.

And then, one day, the group received a package of books from the Soviet embassy in Pyongyang, including two volumes (in Russian) of *Das Kapital*, by Karl Marx, the influential work of political and economic theory that inspired the growth of communism.

One of Blake's fellow prisoners of war was Captain Vyvyan Holt, the only other captive who understood Russian. Holt's eyeglasses had been crushed in an American air raid, so Blake read the entire book out loud, over weeks and months of confinement in a small Korean farmhouse.

The experience of reading *Das Kapital*, Blake said, "turned me from a man of conventional political views, and in the real meaning of the word, a militant anticommunist, into a fervent supporter of the movement I hitherto had been fighting."

Blake was far from alone in feeling the pull of communist ideas. Followers of communism could be found in nearly every country. Communist political parties jostled for position in France, Italy, the Netherlands, Sweden, Finland, and elsewhere. For intellectuals, journalists, and millions of workers, a future without capitalism seemed real and attainable. "People discussed, disputed, and imagined alternative political and economic orders," wrote the historian Melvyn Leffler.

Later on, some people accused Blake of turning to communism for opportunistic reasons, as a way out of the prison camp. But it appears that his conversion was genuine, and its ingredients included the early influence of his cousin, Henri; his deep study of communism and Marx while a prisoner; and above all his disgust at the war and his anger at what he perceived to be America's indiscriminate violence against North Korea.

Blake kept his conversion to the communist cause a secret, but he knew that someday he had to act on it.

In the fall of 1952, his moment came.

One night, when the rest of the prisoners were sleeping, Blake approached the North Korean guardhouse, carrying a note written in Russian, asking for a meeting at the Russian embassy in Pyongyang. Blake promised that he had information they would find interesting.

"I put my finger to my lips as I handed him a folded note," Blake recounted. The guard looked at him with surprise "but took it without saying anything."

Six weeks passed and the Russians hadn't responded.

Then, one morning, a North Korean officer summoned Blake to accompany him to a village nearly an hour's walk away.

The area had been almost completely flattened by American bombers. The officer led Blake into one of the only buildings standing, where "a big, burly man of about forty or forty-five with a pale complexion" greeted him in Russian. That man was the local head of the KGB. Blake's note had fallen into the right hands.

What Blake could not know was that the KGB agent, Nikolai Loenko, had been watching him for months, hoping to draw him into conversation. "George stood out from the motley crew in the camp," Loenko recalled. "He was intelligent, spellbinding. I knew in my bones that here was an opportunity to do some work. I needed only some kind of pretext to make contact with him."

Over weeks of secret interviews, Blake and the KGB came to an agreement: He would provide the Soviet Union with information about any MI6 espionage operations, whether against Russia or its allies. A true convert to the communist cause, Blake insisted that he would not accept money from the Russians.

George Blake had become that most dangerous variety of spy: the double agent. He would soon prove how much damage a single secret agent could inflict on an enemy superpower.

★ ★ ★

The Royal Air Force plane carrying six former POWs from Korea touched down at Abingdon Airfield in England in April 1953. They were the first British prisoners to return home, almost three years since most of them had been trapped during the opening days of the Korean War.

The plane door opened, and George Blake appeared at the top of the staircase, looking out over the large crowd of reporters and well-wishers gathered to welcome him home. A choir struck up a hymn. In the crowd, dignitaries—including the archbishop of Canterbury—cheered as Blake descended. His mother rushed forward and kissed him.

MI6 invited Blake to London for a gentle interrogation about his years as a prisoner. After several days, it was clear that no one suspected Blake of anything other than heroism. "Having been through a rather unusual experience for an SIS officer, few of whom have ever fallen into enemy hands, I found myself, for a short while, a bit of a celebrity," Blake said. Moreover, he was even offered a new job at the spy agency—this time at headquarters.

But first, the chief of MI6 himself, known simply as "C" inside the service, granted Blake several months' vacation to recuperate. George soon left with his mother on a trip to Holland, to visit relatives they had not seen since World War II.

Only Blake and a lone KGB agent knew his real agenda for returning to his birthplace. The trip was "cover," arranged months in advance in North Korea, for the first-ever contact between the spy and his new KGB handler away from the prying eyes of MI6.

Once in the Netherlands, Blake came up with an excuse to make a brief detour to The Hague, a small Dutch city on the North Sea, very close to Rotterdam. He had memorized his instructions: Carrying a local newspaper, the *Nieuwe Rotterdamse Courant*, in his right hand, he walked slowly to a small square at the end of a long boulevard. A man carrying the same newspaper sat on a park bench in the square.

Blake knew his contact only as Korovin. His real name was Nikolai Borisovich Rodin, the Russian spy agency's *rezident*, or top agent in England. Blake sat with Rodin on the bench and described his arrival in England and debriefing by MI6. The two spies then went over procedures for future meetings in London and for setting into motion Blake's new career as a Soviet "mole" inside MI6.

To the KGB, Blake was henceforth known by his code name: DIOMID, or "diamond."

After twenty minutes, Blake returned to Rotterdam, using the back roads he had learned as a teenager in the Dutch resistance. "I was quite sure by now that I was not being followed," Blake recalled. But years later, working at MI6 headquarters, Blake requested Korovin's file and discovered, to his horror, that a British surveillance team— who at the time did not have orders to track Blake, who remained above suspicion—had followed the KGB agent from London all the way to Holland. Fortunately, Korovin had managed to shake his pursuers before his meeting with Blake. "There was much speculation [in Korovin's file] of what the purpose of the trip to Holland could have been," Blake recalled. "I could have told them the answer."

★ ★ ★

Back in London, Blake slipped quietly into his new routine of spying on England for the KGB—all the while pretending to spy on the Soviets for MI6.

Because Rodin was known to MI6, the Soviets assigned Blake a new KGB contact, Sergei Kondrachev, who worked in the Soviet embassy in London as a junior official in charge of cultural events. Kondrachev organized chess competitions and planned tours for famous Soviet musicians— activities that offered the perfect excuse for traveling about the city, scouting out quiet meeting spots, and arranging clandestine rendezvous with DIOMID. Kondrachev was the only Soviet official in London who knew Blake's actual identity or his role in British intelligence.

Only a few weeks into his new assignment, a chilling reminder of the risks of Blake's double life landed on his desk. News arrived at MI6 headquarters in Carlton Gardens that Melinda Maclean, the wife of the Soviet spy Donald Maclean, had disappeared, perhaps seeking to join her defector husband in Moscow. Blake's supervisors ordered him to look for evidence of what happened to her, as talk of treason swirled around the MI6 headquarters. One slip,

Blake knew, and he could be next. "It was too near to the bone," he recalled, "and made me very uncomfortable."

Both Blake and Kondrachev used careful tradecraft: changing their meeting spots constantly; following different, circuitous routes through London; and always signaling that the coast was clear, generally by holding a specific newspaper under the left arm. Blake's Soviet case officer went to extreme lengths to make sure that he was not being tailed by British and American agents.

Kondrachev had come from Moscow, where as a KGB agent he kept watch on US embassy personnel, trailing them throughout the city. He had schooled himself in American evasion techniques—and put them to his own use. "In order to meet me at seven o'clock in the evening," Blake recalled, "he left his house at eight in the morning and was on the move all day. The operation involved several people and cars and a few safe houses. It was difficult and time consuming, but it worked every time." Kondrachev would approach carefully, and "in his grey, soft felt hat and smart grey raincoat he seemed almost part of the fog," Blake remarked.

At this time, Blake also started dating a young secretary in the MI6 office named Gillian Allan, whose father was an MI6 colonel. Like many people who encountered Blake in the weeks and months after his return from Korea, Allan found herself smitten by the young war hero. "He was very charming, very nice, and very considerate and very easy to work for," she said. "He took life very easily, it seemed to me; probably after being in prison for so long he didn't take it as seriously as someone else might have done." The two soon married.

"This was the sort of marriage that SIS welcomed," George Blake commented, because "it kept everything nicely in the family and avoided the strains that can occur when an officer marries 'outside.'" Another family approved of Blake's marriage as well: The KGB believed that Gillian Allan provided the perfect cover for DIOMID, shielding him from any suspicion of being a double agent. They were undoubtedly correct.

★ ★ ★

Blake quickly proved his worth to the KGB, providing Kondrachev with lists of Soviet officials whose phones had been tapped by British intelligence and critical information about other secret operations against Soviet embassies around the world.

The KGB gave Blake a Minox miniature camera, which he carried into his Carlton Gardens office in the back pocket of his pants. Blake was a poor photographer, and it took him some time to learn how to make clear images of the secret documents requested by the Soviets. Eventually, though, "it became automatic. I was almost reduced to a mystical state, when I was the eye and the finger." He was soon photographing reams of classified MI6 documents and passing them on to Kondrachev.

Only two years after Blake's return to London, MI6 transferred him to its espionage station in Berlin. The espionage war with the KGB had taken center stage, and MI6 was determined to send its best agents against the communist foe. It was a move that had fateful consequences, not only for Blake but for the two superpowers who continued their battle of nerves in the war-ravaged city. George Blake's assignment from MI6 was to recruit Soviets to become double agents for the British. Blake, the Soviet double agent, was thus tasked with "turning" his fellow KGB agents to work for his enemy (who also happened to be his employers).

Berlin did make one thing much simpler for Blake. He could meet with his KGB handlers with ease, since, as far as MI6 was concerned, meeting with Soviet agents was part of Blake's job. "This was just one more clandestine meeting among several in a day," he said, "and the danger that I would be caught out was not very great."

Blake soon established a familiar routine, bringing reels of film to his KGB contact in the Soviet sector of the city. The reels contained pictures of thousands of classified British documents. The streets of Berlin, many of which were still lined with abandoned homes and devoid of pedestrians, provided Blake with the cover he needed to hand off such precious—and treacherous—cargo. At an appointed time, a black car would pull alongside him as he walked along a quiet street. "I quickly jumped in,"

Blake recalled, "and was driven at high speed to a safe flat in the neighborhood of Karlshorst," the main Soviet military and KGB compound in East Berlin.

"After an hour or so of leisurely conversation in complete security," Blake said, "I was taken back to the center of town and dropped off in the vicinity of a U-Bahn station. Ten minutes later I was back in West Berlin."

★ ★ ★

Blake's handlers inside the KGB went to great lengths to shield him from MI6's counterespionage teams, who were always on the lookout for traitors and double agents within their ranks. Eventually, the KGB came up with a scheme that would serve as a kind of smoke screen for Blake's spying on behalf of Russia.

"For some time," Blake said, "my Soviet contact and I had been discussing the possibility of planting a genuine Soviet official on me whom I would eventually recruit as a full-blown, conscious agent [for MI6]"—that is, the KGB would make it look like Blake had lured in a high-level Russian official who was willing to hand over Soviet secrets to the British. The official's name was Boris. He knew nothing about Blake's real identity, but neither was he a genuine informer; the KGB worked carefully with him to feed Blake documents and other bogus intelligence, which Blake then gave to MI6. Boris, according to Blake, was the "feather in his cap," earning him accolades inside the British spy agency and deflecting any remote suspicion that Blake might be working for the enemy.

George Blake's career as the KGB's most successful deep-penetration agent was wrapped in such carefully orchestrated deceptions. The secrets surrounding DIOMID were like layers of armor, protecting the KGB's most valuable asset in its secret war against the West.

★ ★ ★

George Blake had entered adulthood as a warrior against Nazism and emerged from World War II an English soldier and patriot. But the Cold War created new and unfamiliar battlefields, for both Blake and millions of other soldiers and citizens around the world. At a distance, the war between East and West—between communism and democracy—might have seemed like a simple choice between good and evil, black and white. On the scorched middle ground of Korea, however, Blake discovered the gray zone, where even hardened loyalties were tested and new alliances forged. Few people could tolerate the gray zone for long, but this was the place where George Blake found his true calling—and his real powers as a spy.

The path of the double agent was lonely and perilous. But as the spy wars in Berlin reached a new phase, the world would learn just how powerful a weapon the spy George Blake would turn out to be.

An East German armored car guards the border crossing between East and West Berlin at the Brandenburg Gate, August 1961.

German Federal Archive

PART **2**

DEEP FREEZE

4

CAPITAL OF THE COLD WAR

The top American spy in Berlin, a city known as a "nest of spies," could be spotted a mile away. William Harvey was an "American James Bond," in the words of Edward Lansdale—himself one of the most storied CIA operatives of the Cold War. But Harvey didn't look the part. Even one of his admirers described him as "odd looking, with protruding eyes and a pear-shaped body. His voice was like that of a bullfrog; once you heard it—and the intellect behind it—you never forgot it."

Others offered less charitable impressions, dubbing Harvey "a bloated alcoholic with the manners of a comically corrupt cop." George Blake once referred to Harvey as a "Texan" with a "Wild West approach to intelligence."

Harvey kept a pearl-handled revolver on his desk. He carried it with him everywhere, even into foreign embassies. "Look," he was known to say, "when you need 'em, you need 'em in a hurry."

Like so many of the spies who fought the secret war between America and Russia, Harvey's outward appearance concealed a very different person. His rough, loud-mouthed ways belied a serious, hard-charging approach to life—and to espionage. Born in Danville, Indiana, in 1915, Harvey's upbringing was a world away from the elite childhoods of most CIA officials, a fact he was conscious of throughout his career. He finished high school at the top of his class at age fifteen and went on to Indiana University in the early days of the Great Depression. He then attended law school and, following graduation, opened a small law practice while still in his early twenties. In 1939, when Adolf Hitler invaded Poland—a shocking event that helped trigger World War II—Harvey decided that he needed to do something bigger with his life, and to "get involved," in the words of his biographer.

A year before Japan attacked Pearl Harbor, Bill Harvey signed up with the FBI. The ambitious small-town boy from Indiana was about to be pulled onto a much larger stage and into a life that he could scarcely have imagined when he first arrived in Washington, DC, to report for training.

During World War II, Bill Harvey fought his battles on the home front, leading counterespionage campaigns against the Abwehr, spies that Hitler sent across the Atlantic to sabotage the American war effort. By 1945, as the war ended, Harvey's spying career was just getting started. That fall, the FBI assigned Harvey to a three-man team tasked with countering Soviet intelligence operations in the United States, a job that soon found him investigating Elizabeth Bentley's revelations of Communist infiltration of the government. Even in those early postwar years, Harvey distinguished himself with "an excellent knowledge of Russian espionage and Communist activities," according to a former colleague.

In 1947, Harvey's life took a sudden, unexpected turn. While still working for the FBI, he attended a party in Washington one evening and had too much to drink (a habit he was known for). He woke up the next morning in his car, having slept the whole night while parked in Rock Creek Park, a wooded area that snaked through the center of the city. His wife, Libby, had called the Bureau, looking for him. When FBI director J. Edgar Hoover—who did not tolerate recklessness in his bureau—heard what had happened, he fired Harvey on the spot.

Fortunately for Harvey, a new employer in Washington

was looking for recruits. The Central Intelligence Agency was created in September 1947, its mission to combine all the nation's overseas intelligence operations under one roof. In those early years, the CIA was small and poorly organized and overshadowed by the much larger FBI and US Army (which included a number of intelligence departments). Far from being under one physical roof, the CIA's staff was scattered among office buildings all over Washington, DC, many of them drafty, temporary structures built during World War II.

The "Agency," in short, was a place of opportunity for anyone hungry to get in the game of espionage in the late 1940s. Harvey fit the bill perfectly, and the CIA scooped him up immediately. His recklessness served him well in an environment where risk taking, and a willingness to break the rules, earned him accolades. By 1951, Harvey had managed to scramble all the way to the top of the CIA's hierarchy, becoming the head of counterintelligence in just four years. Daring, larger-than-life Bill Harvey was now America's top spy hunter—and he was determined to make his mark in the war against communism.

Harvey landed in Berlin in the fall of 1952, three years ahead of George Blake. He quickly settled into the Berlin Operating Base (known by the acronym "BOB"), which was housed in a small villa in Dahlem, on the outskirts of the city. The house had once been owned by General Ludwig Beck, who had been executed by the Nazis for his role in an assassination attempt on Adolf Hitler in 1944. From this modest, cramped perch, Harvey conjured up big plans for the CIA's secret war against the communist enemy.

Harvey could not have picked a better place. The former German capital sat deep inside the zone of Soviet occupation, in the eastern part of Germany. Surrounded on all sides by the Red Army and by units of the KGB, West Berlin floated like an island in a hostile, turbulent sea. In other words, it was the perfect spot for America and its allies to spy on the Soviets.

That same winter, a new American president, General Dwight D. Eisenhower, proclaimed to Americans, "We sense with all our faculties that forces of good and evil are massed and armed and opposed as rarely before in history....Freedom is pitted against slavery; lightness against the dark." In Moscow, Stalin's successor, Nikita Khrushchev, spoke with equal conviction about the advantages of communism and the Soviet system. Like many of his countrymen, the Soviet leader believed that communism had set his country on a path toward social justice and modernization; its triumph over capitalism was all but inevitable. "Whether you like it or not," he said, "history is on our side. We will bury you."

Whatever middle ground was left between the two sides was melting away, and more than anywhere else, Berlin symbolized this widening gulf. Over seventy million cubic meters of rubble left over from the war still marred the city's landscape. Vacant buildings, many of them pockmarked with bullet holes, lined half-deserted streets. The Brandenburg Gate, a monument to the city's former greatness, still stood in the middle of the city, in the midst of a no-man's-land between East and West.

Officially, four occupying powers divided the city into Soviet, American, British, and French sectors. But in reality, an invisible line ran down the middle of Berlin, separating the communist East from the capitalist West. East German guards kept watch over random checkpoints, demanding identity papers for anyone wishing to pass through. Yet people managed to move from one sector to the other, day after day, making Berlin the one place on earth where America and Russia—and their spies—came into contact.

Only seven years earlier, fresh from their victory over Hitler, American and Russian leaders—and most of their citizens—believed that the two nations could coexist in peace. By 1952, that notion had evaporated. As Harvey settled into the house in Dahlem, the Cold War between America and the Soviet Union threatened to break into open hostility. In this terrifying new context, the demand for hard intelligence about the communist enemy became more urgent than ever.

Bill Harvey's CIA, once a haphazard agency with a handful of offices in Washington, DC, was now adding more and more recruits and was quickly assembling a worldwide network of "stations," from Hong Kong to Cairo. The Agency was still smaller than its Russian counterpart, and its agents had to train hard to learn the techniques of spycraft—which Soviet operatives had been mastering for decades. But each month, new agents posing as businesspeople, diplomats, professors, and other unassuming characters quietly joined the fight against the Soviet Union.

More of them arrived in Berlin than anywhere else.

Maneuvering silently through the streets of Germany's demolished capital city—sometimes referred to as the "capital of the Cold War"—the CIA and its main adversary, the KGB, jockeyed for advantage on Bill Harvey's new battlefield.

★ ★ ★

Bill Harvey knew that for all the CIA's efforts, a big question hung over its attempts to look deep inside the Soviet power structure. By that point, nearly every effort to send a US agent behind the Iron Curtain had failed; the KGB was simply too well entrenched and too vigilant for the Americans to sneak past its nets. And while it was true that VENONA cracked the Soviets' secret codes and peered into their most heavily protected communications, that victory was spoiled by one simple fact. The VENONA cables had been intercepted during World War II, nearly a decade earlier. The information they contained was out of date—hardly the fresh intelligence on Soviet activities that President Eisenhower clamored for. What was the CIA's next big move going to be?

The answer sat just over the border, in Berlin's Soviet sector.

Through a carefully cultivated network of German informers, Bill Harvey learned that Berlin held the key to Europe's communications networks—the very networks used by the Soviets to communicate between Moscow and its enormous military bases in East Germany. The city's cable-switching stations acted like the hub of a giant wheel, whose spokes spread out across the entire continent. But by a quirk of geography, all of the city's telephone and telegraph stations (where the lines connected and where messages were routed by operators) lay in the Soviet sector.

Harvey's agents managed to cultivate informants working inside the East German telecommunications offices, in order to find out which cables were used directly by the Soviet army and secret services. One informant was code-named NUMMER MÄDCHEN, or "numbers girl." This informant—whose identity remains unknown to this day—provided the CIA with precious information about who was using which cables and when. Another informant, a lawyer for the East German Ministry of Posts and Communications, secretly copied information about Soviet cables to paper cards, which he then taped to his backside, underneath his pants. When he met with his CIA contacts, he would excuse himself briefly to lower his pants and retrieve the notes.

The CIA found the precise spot in East Berlin where the communications cables could be tapped—only it was a site inside Soviet territory, where Soviet soldiers and East German police (the Volkspolizei, or VoPos) watched every move.

Harvey had an idea. If American and British engineers could build an underground tunnel long enough and somehow reach the cables from below, then the Soviets would have no idea that the United States was listening in. Nothing this big, this daring, or this expensive had ever been attempted by a spy service.

A memo sent to Allen Dulles, the director of Central Intelligence, argued that BOB could get access to the Soviet communications network "through the construction of a subterranean passage approximately 1,800 feet in length, one half of which will be in Soviet territory." Dulles, who immediately grasped the potential for tapping into the Soviets' secret communications, approved the plan immediately.

The tunnel was called Operation Gold, but the massive project quickly earned a nickname: "Harvey's Hole." It soon grew, thanks to Harvey's stubborn determination, into the largest and most expensive espionage operation ever launched by the CIA.

Operation Gold began in the summer of 1954 with the construction of a drab-looking warehouse sitting just over the boundary separating East and West Berlin. Only a handful of people in the CIA and MI6 knew about the operation. Harvey ordered a delicate and highly classified operation to keep the small construction site totally secret from prying eyes, going so far as to assign watchers to keep records of all pedestrians and cars in the neighborhood, in case a KGB surveillance team might be snooping about. The warehouse was made to look like one of the many Allied radar facilities in Berlin at that time; even the engineers and other CIA personnel who came and went wore the uniforms of the US Army Signal Corps, pretending to be radar operators. CIA operatives placed tiny microphones in the neighborhood around the warehouse and along the fence, where the Volkspolizei patrolled day and night—listening out for any signs that someone suspected that a major operation was under way. Bill Harvey was relieved to learn that they picked up no inkling of suspicion near the site.

To excavate the tunnel, the CIA brought in the Army Corps of Engineers, the military agency responsible for some of the century's most celebrated engineering feats, from containing the Mississippi River to building air bases in Korea in record time. The corps first built a mock-up of the tunnel, several hundred feet long, in the Nevada desert. The soils beneath Berlin were sandy and unstable;

engineers quickly determined that the entire length of the 1,800-foot tunnel had to be sheathed in steel, to prevent the structure from collapsing.

Despite these daunting conditions, the scale of the operation quickly grew into an enormous enterprise. Hundreds of steel cylinders, each of them six feet in diameter, were manufactured specially in Virginia and then transported by ship to the West German port of Bremerhaven. Hidden in wooden crates, they were then loaded onto trains that had to pass through communist East Germany—and risk being detected—before reaching the American sector in Berlin. A single cylinder weighed 125 tons. All of them arrived safely, and secretly, at the Operation Gold warehouse.

Harvey's team started digging in September 1954. Over the next four months, they removed more than 3,000 tons of sand and soil, carefully inserting steel rings into the tunnel as they dug beneath Berlin's streets. Each night, the construction crews emerged from the tunnel covered in mud and construction debris. Leaving the building in this condition might attract attention to them, so Harvey had a washing machine and dryer installed in the warehouse.

For four months, Operation Gold remained completely undercover.

By February 1955, the tunnel was nearly done—complete with its own ventilation system and trolley for moving men and matériel along the full length of the narrow passageway.

In the final days of the operation, Harvey's men hollowed out a "tap room" immediately beneath the Russian communications cables, where they installed technical equipment specially designed to receive the electronic signals siphoned from the cables and transmit them via wire through the length of the tunnel. They worked dangerously close to the surface of the ground. Occasionally, the hobnailed boots of East German soldiers, patrolling the street above, echoed overhead.

At last, technicians reached the Soviet cables, carefully exposing the inner wires and grafting on the wiretaps. Bill Harvey's gamble was about to pay off.

Beginning that very month, Harvey's wiretap commenced recording thousands of classified conversations among Soviet and East German military officials. Three times a week, his team packed up huge quantities of taped voice reels and secreted them by aircraft from Tempelhof Airport in West Berlin to London, where they were then driven to a secure CIA location to be transcribed and analyzed. Hundreds upon hundreds of classified reports flowed out of the project, providing the United States and its allies with their only steady supply of information on Soviet military strength and planning, nuclear capabilities, and technological know-how. It was, in the words of one CIA agent, "a bonanza."

Operation Gold suddenly inundated the CIA and the White House with daily updates of everything from the names of thousands of key Soviet officers to the location of Soviet air force bases in Eastern Europe and the Soviet Union, and the location and size of the Soviet navy's Baltic Fleet, which patrolled the North Atlantic. Amazingly, too, the Berlin Tunnel tap revealed the names of hundreds of top GRU (Soviet military intelligence) officers working in East Germany, creating a wealth of new espionage targets for the CIA and MI6. In all, the wiretap in "Harvey's Hole" recorded a staggering 433,000 conversations, giving America insight into the mind and plans of its main enemy.

★ ★ ★

In the middle of the night on April 22, 1956, American agents guarding the Berlin Tunnel warehouse observed movement on the street located just above the tap site, in the Soviet sector. Peering through their night-vision equipment, they saw teams of men digging holes.

They quickly alerted Harvey that something was amiss. Harvey rushed into the tunnel, to do what he could to protect his creation.

An hour later, Russian speech could be heard through the microphone in the tap chamber. By the next morning, East German and Russian technicians had pushed all the way through to the eastern end of the tunnel itself.

"Look at that," one of them was heard saying. "It goes all the way under the highway! How did they do it? It's fantastic!"

Working methodically—and filming everything with movie cameras—the Soviets and East Germans finally reached the halfway point of the tunnel, where Harvey had set up a barrier of barbed wire and sandbags. A hand-lettered sign, in German and Russian, read: YOU ARE NOW ENTERING THE AMERICAN SECTOR.

Modeled after the border crossings above ground, the sign was perhaps meant as a joke among spies. But when footsteps could be heard moving past that point, Harvey issued a sterner warning: Manning a .50-caliber machine gun himself, he pulled back the bolt, which made a noise that the intruders recognized instantly. They retreated, quickly, to the Soviet side.

Eleven months and eleven days after it was first launched, Operation Gold shut down for good.

Despite its being unmasked by the Soviets, Operation Gold secured Harvey's reputation inside the CIA as one of its wiliest and smartest operatives. America's leaders celebrated the Berlin Tunnel as one of the CIA's clearest victories in the Cold War—and evidence of the West's superior technological capabilities and spycraft. It finally seemed as if the CIA could breach the Iron Curtain.

Bill Harvey spent the next three years in Berlin building BOB into a formidable base of operations for America's secret campaign against Russia. When he finally returned to CIA headquarters in 1959, Director Allen Dulles awarded Harvey the Distinguished Intelligence Medal, in recognition of his victories in Berlin. And then Dulles handed Harvey a plum: control of Division D, putting him in charge of the CIA's covert operations around the world.

★ ★ ★

Back in Berlin, Bill Harvey's carefully nurtured network of informants continued to reap new intelligence rewards for the Americans.

On January 4, 1961, one of BOB's most tantalizing leads was about to pay off. For months, an anonymous source, code-named SNIPER (or Heckenschuetze), had been supplying the CIA with tidbits of information about Soviet and East German spies in Berlin. It was information only a highly placed insider could have acquired. Bill Harvey's successor as the head of BOB, David Murphy, was eager to bring SNIPER "in from the cold" and figure out whether he was the real thing—and to see what more he might divulge.

BOB gave SNIPER a special telephone number to dial to arrange a clandestine meeting; their superiors warned the switchboard operators that "if they missed his call they would be on the next boat home."

The switchboard lit up at five thirty PM: SNIPER was on his way. "The excitement at BOB was palpable," one participant recalled. A taxi arrived a half hour later, and two people emerged, a man and a woman. SNIPER had arrived, with his girlfriend.

SNIPER revealed himself as Lieutenant Colonel Michal Goleniewski, the former second in command of Polish military counterintelligence and a high-level KGB source. Once his identity was established, the CIA spirited Goleniewski away to a safe house and eventually to Washington, where he handed over hundreds of names of Soviet and Eastern Bloc spies to the Americans. As Goleniewski ticked off the names of some of the KGB's closely guarded secret agents, there was jubilation inside the Agency, as it seemed like the United States had scored yet another major victory in the spy wars against Russia.

Golienewski then revealed a secret from the KGB's inner sanctum. The CIA's celebrations stopped.

SNIPER explained to his dumbfounded interrogators that the Soviets had been running a double agent inside MI6, code-named DIOMID. This mole had provided the KGB with detailed knowledge of the very operation that Bill Harvey had worked for months to keep hidden. Operation Gold had been blown before the first shovel of soil had been removed from "Harvey's Hole." What's more, the mole's real name was familiar to any spy who had served in Berlin during Bill Harvey's heyday there: For DIOMID, as America now learned, was George Blake.

MI5 agents immediately arrested Blake in London, and he quickly confessed to spying for the Russians.

The CIA determined that Blake had passed over 4,000 documents to the Soviets, many of them containing highly classified information about British and American spies. But it was Blake's detailed knowledge of Operation Gold that threw Bill Harvey's CIA colleagues into disarray. Suddenly, everything they thought they knew about their successes and failures in Berlin seemed topsy-turvy.

Was the KGB's discovery of the Berlin Tunnel a charade? And if that was true, what about all the thousands of pages of secret intelligence gathered by the CIA through the tapped cables? Was all of that information tainted or manipulated by the Soviets to mislead the Americans and their allies? Where did the truth lie? Deep inside the CIA, these questions sowed confusion and mistrust among the Agency's most senior agents and leaders. To many of his fellow agents, Bill Harvey's gold mine suddenly seemed like a mirage.

★ ★ ★

At his sentencing for treason in a London courtroom, George Blake was given one year in prison for each of the British agents he was known to have betrayed to the Soviet Union: forty-two. It was the longest prison sentence in modern British history.

But George Blake's espionage career didn't come to an end on the day he was led in shackles to Wormwood Scrubs prison, outside London. For the next five years, Blake schemed a way to escape the high walls and drab food of "the Scrubs," as it was called by the inmates. His plan drew on all the skills he had learned as a spy.

The former double agent now morphed into the model prisoner, charming the Scrubs' guards and administrators and making friends among its inmates. Time became his ally, as inside the prison memories slowly faded of Blake's treachery outside the walls, and Wormwood Scrubs came to view George Blake as a helpful and harmless middle-aged man. All the while, Blake kept watch for weaknesses in the prison's perimeter. He found them, but he would need help getting out.

As it happened, Blake forged close relationships with three men willing to play supporting roles in his escape. Michael Randle and Pat Pottle were peace activists who had been given prison sentences for their antiwar protests in England. Sean Bourke, a troubled man with a criminal past, viewed helping Blake as a way to get back at the police. All three had come to the end of their sentences and would soon be released.

After he left prison, Bourke visited Blake and managed

to smuggle a walkie-talkie to him. At night, Bourke would sneak close to the walls to communicate with Blake, who could only whisper into the device. Several weeks later, they had settled on an escape plan.

At the appointed time, on a rainy evening when all the other inmates were enjoying a movie in the prison auditorium, George Blake removed part of an old window that looked out over the prison yard. He squeezed through the opening, lowered himself to the ground, and dashed across the open space to the wall. On the other side, Sean Bourke idled in a getaway car on a deserted street. Hearing Blake's signal, he tossed a homemade nylon rope ladder over the wall. When Blake was sure that no one was watching, he scrambled up the ladder and dropped to the ground on the other side. Blake stepped into the waiting car, and the two men drove off into the night.

With the help of Randle, Pottle, and Bourke, George Blake hid in England for the next two months, moving from house to house. His prison break made international news. British newspapers splashed his face on their covers, making it impossible for him to show himself anywhere in public. Getting out of England was going to be his only hope of eluding the British authorities.

Betting that his former KGB friends would offer him refuge, Blake devised a plan to escape to the East. Once again, his fate depended on the help of friends: Randle and Pottle converted part of a Dormobile (a small British camper van) into a secret compartment that could just barely fit a single person.

Soon after, Michael Randle; his wife, Anne; and their two young boys boarded the ferry from Dover, England, to Ostend, Belgium, on the first leg of a family trip across Europe, with a secret cargo crammed uncomfortably in the rear of their camper.

Twenty hours after the Randles left England, George Blake emerged from their Dormobile exhausted but exhilarated. They had crossed safely into East Germany and reached the outskirts of Berlin, the city's lights visible in the distance. Not wanting to attract attention, Blake and his friends parted quietly. "For an instant in time I was free and alone in the dark night," he recalled, "poised between two worlds, belonging to neither." George Blake stepped forward, out of the gray zone of the double agent, and chose to make the communist East his home.

The Soviet Union welcomed George Blake as a hero. He went on to have a celebrated career as a Soviet intelligence instructor and was sought after as an expert on Western espionage tactics. At the time of this writing, he is ninety-six and living in a cottage outside Moscow, where he regularly receives guests and admirers (including Russian president Vladimir Putin, himself a former KGB agent).

★　★　★

Late at night on August 13, 1961, East German police and military units flooded the streets of Berlin's Eastern sector. They pulled up train tracks and blocked roads. Construction crews stretched barbed-wire fencing across the entire twenty-seven-mile border separating East from West Berlin, and also around the entire ninety-seven-mile circumference of West Berlin itself. By morning, the small garrison of American and allied forces could only watch as all of West Berlin was sealed off.

Closing the border between East and West Berlin was not the idea of the KGB, the Soviet army, or anyone in the Kremlin: It was the brainchild of Walter Ulbricht, East Germany's hard-line communist leader. For Ulbricht, the problem with the city's open border had nothing to do with spies: It was with the dissatisfaction of his own people, the seventeen million citizens of the German Democratic Republic, or GDR. Between 1949 and 1961, one out of every six East Germans had fled the GDR, escaping to the freedoms—and increasingly, the prosperity—of the West. These three million people included teachers, engineers, doctors, scientists, and intellectuals. East Germany's most skilled and talented people voted with their feet, choosing to rebuild from scratch rather than adjust to life under communism.

With each passing year, the refugee numbers increased. In 1960, 500 people left East Germany every single day; that year, more than 180,000 people made the trek from

East to West. And most of them crossed the border at its softest point, in Berlin.

As he walked by a shop in East Berlin one day, the East German spy chief Markus Wolf overheard a woman complaining that "they can launch the *Sputnik*, but you can't get a green vegetable in the middle of summer. That's socialism for you." For his part, Walter Ulbricht understood perfectly well what was at stake. "The booming economy in West Germany, which is visible to every citizen of the GDR, is the primary reason that in the last ten years around two million people have left our republic," Ulbricht wrote in a letter to the Soviet leader. "We are a state," he continued, "which stands with open borders at the center of the competition between two world systems."

Unless that border could be closed off completely, Ulbricht believed, the GDR was bound to lose.

In the days that followed August 13, construction workers toiled day and night to replace the barbed wire with a permanent wall. VoPo units looked on, menacing anyone attempting to slip through. The East German government referred to the structure as the "Anti-Fascist Protection Rampart"; it was bordered by minefields and a no-man's-land known as the "death strip." Border guards shot on sight anyone trying to cross (usually from East to West).

In a single evening, the Communist government of East Germany not only forged the most enduring symbol of the Cold War but also blocked off America's prime source of secret intelligence on its main enemy, the USSR. Berlin's role as the main stage of the espionage wars came to an abrupt end.

★ ★ ★

The construction of the Berlin Wall might well have been a crushing defeat for Bill Harvey and his fellow spies. But long before the Wall went up, the CIA was already scoping out new battlefields in the secret war with the KGB. As a new decade dawned in the Cold War, the struggle between America and Russia was quickly spreading around the globe—and into the skies above.

Francis Gary Powers in his flight suit, standing next to the U-2.

Associated Press

5

THE PILOT

On May 1, 1960, as Soviet citizens rose early to prepare for May Day celebrations all over the USSR, CIA pilot Francis Gary Powers sweltered in his U-2 spy plane, wondering when he would get the takeoff signal. A fellow pilot draped his flight jacket over the U-2's cockpit window, trying to give Powers some relief as the unmarked black aircraft baked in the sun on an airstrip near Peshawar, Pakistan.

Powers had been up since two AM, undergoing medical tests, scarfing down a huge breakfast, and cramming himself into his uncomfortable, pressurized flight suit. For the next thirteen hours, he would not be able to eat, drink, relieve himself, or remove his tight-fitting helmet.

Only a few people inside the CIA and the White House had been informed about Powers's top secret mission, Operation Overflight. He was a new breed of spy: quiet and unassuming, but skilled at handling the equipment that was becoming vital to America's espionage campaign against the Soviets. As the Cold War entered a new decade, knowledge of the enemy had become America's primary strategic goal; according to Richard Bissell, the director of the U-2 program, "ninety percent of our hard intelligence information about the Soviet Union" came from the high-definition cameras mounted on the underbellies of the Agency's spy planes.

By six AM, he'd been sitting in the cockpit's scorching heat for nearly an hour. Finally, at 6:20, word came directly from the White House that takeoff had been approved.

Powers quickly sealed the U-2's canopy. The plane dubbed "the black lady of espionage" by the Soviets revved its engines and started on a 3,788-mile arc over the Soviet Union to a secret base in Bodø, Norway. This was only the latest of many U-2 flights over the USSR. They were a constant irritant to the Soviets, who could only watch and fret as the U-2s soared beyond the reach of their jet fighters and missiles.

Even veteran U-2 pilots like Powers found it thrilling to take off in the powerful jet plane. "Ascent was rapid and spectacular," Powers observed. "The U-2 required very little runway for takeoff; a thousand feet would suffice. Within moments…you could begin climbing—at better than a forty-five-degree angle." The takeoff angle was so steep, and the plane's thrust so powerful, that test pilots felt as though the plane might flip over backward as it rocketed toward altitudes of 70,000 feet, until that point the highest ever reached in the history of aviation.

In addition to his parachute, Powers wore a pack outfitted with survival gear, including emergency food, a hunting knife, and a .22-caliber pistol with a silencer attached. It also held a large cloth, which included the following message, translated into fourteen different languages:

I AM AN AMERICAN AND DO NOT SPEAK YOUR LANGUAGE. I NEED FOOD, SHELTER, ASSISTANCE. I WILL NOT HARM YOU. I BEAR NO MALICE TOWARD YOUR PEOPLE. IF YOU HELP ME, YOU WILL BE REWARDED.

The CIA stashed rubles, gold coins, and even jewelry in the emergency kit for pilots to bargain with in case they were captured.

Beneath Powers's seat, engineers had also installed an explosive charge. If Powers had to eject while in flight, his instructions were first to flip a switch marked ARM and a second switch marked DESTRUCT. He would then have no more than seventy seconds to eject from the plane before it was blown to pieces. The CIA wanted to make sure that no one on the ground could retrieve the plane's sensitive equipment intact.

All of these preparations gave pilots some minor comfort. In fact, CIA officials privately believed that a pilot could never survive a high-altitude ejection from the spy plane. If something went wrong, death was almost certain. "It was a cruel assumption," President Eisenhower said, "but I was assured that the young pilots undertaking these missions were doing so with their eyes open and motivated by a high degree of patriotism, a swashbuckling bravado, and certain material inducement."

Powers's commander, Colonel William Shelton, approached him just before boarding earlier that morning.

"Do you want the silver dollar?" Shelton asked.

The dollar coin was fake and hollowed out. "It looked like a good-luck charm," Powers recalled. "It seemed to be an ordinary silver dollar, with a metal loop at one end so it could be fastened onto a key chain around the neck." Inside, a narrow sheath enclosed a sharp pin treated with a shellfish toxin that could kill a person instantly. The CIA had developed this suicide device at the cost of $3 million. According to Richard Bissell, pilots were "exhorted but not ordered" to use the pin if they were ever captured on Soviet soil.

Powers could choose for himself whether to accept the coin or not; he took it from Shelton and slipped it into his pocket.

★ ★ ★

The idea for a spy plane that could strike deep into Soviet territory had captured the imaginations of CIA planners since the beginning of the Cold War. But with the real possibility of nuclear conflict with the USSR—and the failure of the CIA to send its own agents behind the Iron Curtain—the time had come to make it happen. In late November 1954, CIA director Allen Dulles emerged from a meeting with President Eisenhower with orders to develop a top secret aircraft.

The job was handed to Clarence "Kelly" Johnson, the nation's top aircraft designer and engineer.

At Lockheed Aircraft Corporation in Burbank, California, Johnson had created the "Skunk Works," a secret research-and-development lab hidden from prying eyes by tall barbed-wire fences and blacked-out windows. The Skunk Works (the name was an inside joke, taken from a popular cartoon strip called *Li'l Abner*) became legendary during and after World War II for achieving engineering breakthroughs under almost impossibly tight deadlines. Working under Johnson, Skunk Works engineers designed the first tactical jet fighter (the F-80) and the world's fastest plane (the F-104). However, those firsts would pale in comparison with Johnson's new assignment: The president wanted a plane that could fly high enough to avoid Soviet radar, and far enough to cross the Soviet Union without refueling. And he wanted it right away.

In a feat of modern aircraft design and engineering, Johnson's team built the first U-2 spy plane in only eighty-eight days. By February 1955, a prototype was ready to fly. With powerful jet engines and a wingspan longer than its fuselage, the spy plane was "part jet, part glider," according to Powers. Unarmed and defenseless against enemy fighters or antiaircraft fire, the U-2 was purpose-built to house powerful cameras designed for the CIA by Edwin Land, the founder of the Polaroid Corporation. The cameras were fed by 12,000 feet of film, an astonishing quantity made possible by a thin Mylar strip specially manufactured by Eastman Kodak.

A few months later, a small fleet of U-2 planes began rolling off the Skunk Works assembly lines.

The CIA recruited the Air Force's best pilots to test the U-2. In exchange for lives of secrecy and danger, this small group of men got a chance at real adventure—and, as an added incentive, paychecks that were more than double what they earned as Air Force pilots.

That money was no small thing to Francis Gary Powers, who had grown up the son of a coal miner in Virginia during the Great Depression, in a home with no electricity or running water.

During World War II, Powers's dad paid $2.50 for Francis, then fourteen, to take his first airplane ride, in a single-engine Piper Cub; after landing, Francis told him, "Dad, I left my heart up there."

Francis Gary Powers never let go of his love for flying. After college, in 1951, he immediately signed up with the Air Force. He finished his training just as the Korean War settled into a truce, narrowly missing the chance to fly combat missions. "I hadn't really proved myself," he recalled. That didn't slow Powers down, however, and for the next four years he made up for his lack of wartime experience by training continuously, eventually becoming part of a small corps of the nation's best fighter pilots.

The CIA offered Powers a spot in the top secret U-2 program in January 1956. "I was amazed," he recalled, "and immensely proud, not only for being chosen to participate in such a venture, but, even more, proud of my country itself, for having the courage, and guts, to do what it believed essential, and right."

Powers and his fellow test pilots trained for months at a secret facility in a remote part of the Nevada desert known as Area 51, learning to control the powerful experimental planes. The U-2's huge wings generated so much lift that the plane resisted landing; pilots had to stall the engines just above the runway in the final moments before touchdown. And the spy plane's structure had been designed for stealth, not strength. Once, when a fighter jet accidentally passed too close to a U-2, the spy plane broke up amid the turbulence, and its pilot was instantly killed.

On July 4, 1956, Eisenhower authorized the first secret U-2 flight over the Soviet Union. The plane's high-tech cameras generated a bonanza of intelligence, like nothing the CIA had ever seen. Soon, regular U-2 missions provided Eisenhower and the CIA with razor-sharp images of military bases, missile launching pads, and more. For the first time in the Cold War, American military leaders felt that they had a clear image of Russia's military capabilities—knowledge that would help the United States stay one step ahead of its adversary.

"I was able to get a look at every blade of grass in the Soviet Union," CIA director Allen Dulles said.

★ ★ ★

By the late 1950s, the main focus of the espionage war was moving from the streets of Berlin to the upper reaches of the earth's atmosphere.

In August 1955, Russian rocket scientists announced that they would soon be able to send a satellite into space. On October 4, 1957, they made good on their promise: The Soviet Union launched a rocket into space containing *Sputnik*, a 185-pound satellite capable of orbiting the earth. *Sputnik* weighed three times more than the United States' *Vanguard 1* satellite, which had not even launched successfully. Worse, *Sputnik* proved that the Soviets had developed advanced rocket technology, backing up Khrushchev's recent boasts that the USSR could strike the US mainland with a nuclear weapon.

Less than a month later, the Soviets shot a second satellite into orbit—*Sputnik 2*—carrying a live dog named Laika, suggesting that they might soon develop the ability to send a human into space. Shortly afterward, the United States' own satellite blew up on the launchpad.

If the new "space race" made Americans fear that they were falling behind the Soviets, a new arms race—involving intercontinental ballistic missiles, or ICBMs—added a terrifying new dimension to the Cold War. These ballistic missiles followed an arcing trajectory, piercing the earth's atmosphere and falling to earth with the force of gravity; once launched, they could not be stopped. The first Soviet ICBM flew 3,300 miles in August 1957; the first American ICBM flight took place well over a year later, in November 1958. ICBMs could reach their targets in less than an hour. Americans and Russians now lived with the real possibility that nuclear war might happen at any time, and with almost no warning.

Both nations scrambled to build more missiles and to devise clever, and lethal, ways of launching them at the enemy. Only two months after *Sputnik*, the US Navy ordered the construction of the USS *George Washington*, the world's first nuclear-armed submarine. When it launched on June 9, 1959, the stealthy sub carried sixteen nuclear-tipped missiles capable of hurling a warhead 1,300 miles. Each of these missiles carried a warhead equal in destructive power to forty Little Boys—or forty times the bomb dropped on Hiroshima.

The United States had 370 nuclear weapons in 1950. A decade later, that number had skyrocketed to more than 40,000 warheads and bombs. And from only a handful in 1950, the Soviet nuclear arsenal had grown to more than 3,000 weapons in 1960—many fewer than the United States, but still enough to destroy America and its allies several times over.

The superpower conflict seemed to take a sudden, more ominous turn: a kind of calculated standoff, in which "winning" now depended on guessing correctly at the enemy's strength and intentions. Who might launch the first missiles? Which country could survive a first strike? The conflict with communism, it seemed, had spiraled into a life-or-death contest, with the fate of the earth hanging in the balance.

★ ★ ★

President Eisenhower watched these developments and found himself deeply troubled. He had served as supreme commander of Allied Expeditionary Forces during World War II and had witnessed firsthand the destruction of Europe. The threat of a new, more destructive conflict weighed heavily on him. Moreover, despite the rising global tensions with the USSR, the United States was enjoying one of the most prosperous decades in its history. Eisenhower worried about the impact of military spending on the budget of the US government and feared it could crowd out other priorities and eventually stall America's roaring economic growth.

In the fall of 1959, seeking to ease tensions with his rival, Eisenhower invited Khrushchev to make the first-ever visit by a Soviet leader to the United States. Khrushchev toured Washington, visited a farm in Iowa, and even watched a movie being filmed in Hollywood. Khrushchev relished the attention. "Who would have thought that the capitalists would invite me, a worker?" Khrushchev confided to his son Sergei.

Before Khrushchev's departure, in a rare moment of warmth and cooperation, Eisenhower and Khrushchev agreed to hold summit talks in Paris the following May, where they would hammer out an agreement to reduce their stockpiles of nuclear weapons. Later that fall, in Moscow, Khrushchev declared that "the clouds of war have begun to disperse."

Privately, Eisenhower began to dread what might happen if the U-2 program were exposed to the world, or the impact such a revelation might have on his new overtures to the Soviet leader. "If one of these planes is shot down," he said, "this thing is going to be on my head. I'm going to catch hell. The whole world will be in a mess."

Francis Gary Powers's U-2 plane crossed into Soviet airspace just six days before the start of the Paris summit.

★ ★ ★

Not long after taking off, Powers noticed a Soviet fighter jet flying far beneath him. The U-2 achieved a high altitude that made it impossible for the jet to intercept or shoot at Powers. "I wondered how the Russians felt," he recalled, "knowing I was up here, unable to do anything about it."

In fact, the Soviet military tracked Powers from the moment he had crossed the USSR's border. Enraged by the incursion—coming as it did on the heels of what seemed like a warmer relationship with Eisenhower and the United States—Khrushchev ordered his air defenses to try to shoot the plane down. Before 1960, Soviet antiaircraft missiles had been incapable of reaching the high-flying U-2s. That spring, however, the USSR had begun installing SA-2 missile batteries all over the country, which could potentially strike targets at altitudes higher than 60,000 feet—a capability that, before May 1, had never been tested.

Four hours after his departure, Powers soared over Sverdlovsk, an important industrial city that had never before been photographed by a U-2 plane. He switched on the plane's surveillance cameras, readying them to take their precious, high-altitude photographs. At almost precisely the same moment, a huge orange flash lit up the sky behind him, pitching the plane forward.

"My God, I've had it now," he said out loud.

The next moments were chaos. The U-2's wings broke off. With the plane's nose pointing upward, the fuselage, with Powers still strapped inside, hurtled toward the earth. "All I could see was blue sky," Powers remembered, "spinning, spinning, spinning."

As he reached for the eject button, Powers realized that the plane's centrifugal force was pressing the lower half of his body into the cockpit. He feared that the power of the ejection might shear off his legs.

Powers managed to knock out the plane's canopy and push his body out of the plane. "Suddenly I was free," he remembered, "my body just falling...even better than floating in a swimming pool, I remember thinking." In the frenetic moments following the explosion, he had not managed to arm the self-destruct mechanism.

His parachute popped open automatically. Ten thousand feet above the earth, Powers glided down slowly, the landscape beneath him gradually coming into view. Powers thought of the silver dollar in his pocket, and it suddenly occurred to him that if he were captured, "it was one of the first things they would take." While still in the air, he unscrewed the poison pin, keeping it in its small sheath; he then tossed the silver dollar to the ground below and returned the pin to his pocket. He wanted to keep it just in case—but he was still hopeful of escaping alive.

★ ★ ★

Powers landed hard in a field. A farmer ran up to help him, and a larger group of Russian men arrived in a car, surrounding him as he lay sprawled on the ground. They pulled at his harness and his parachute. Powers could only nod and point as they peppered him with questions in Russian, a language he did not understand at all. His head pounded with pain from the sudden descent, and his heart raced.

In the confusion of those early moments, Powers could not reach his survival gear—including the money and the cloth with its message in fourteen languages. "I was completely unprepared," Powers recalled.

The Russians led Powers to a nearby car, and then drove him along a bumpy, muddy road to what he assumed was a police station. The man sitting next to him in the backseat had found Powers's pistol and removed it from its holster. On the shiny barrel, the letters USA had been clearly etched.

The man asked him in Russian a question that Powers interpreted to mean, "Are you an American?"

"It seemed useless to deny it," Powers recalled. Hours

later, Soviet officials met him at the police station and then hustled him onto a small airplane bound for Moscow.

★ ★ ★

News that Powers had not landed as planned in Norway jolted the CIA, and the president was alerted immediately that the U-2 spy plane had almost certainly gone down. At CIA headquarters, Richard Bissell told CIA director Allen Dulles that Powers could not have survived a crash.

On May 3, Eisenhower authorized a false cover story. A press release from the National Aeronautics and Space Administration made this low-key announcement:

A NASA U-2 research airplane being flown in Turkey on a joint NASA-USAF Air Weather Service mission apparently went down in the Lake Van, Turkey, area at about 9:00 A.M. (3:00 A.M. E.D.T.), Sunday, May 1.

American newspapers barely took notice: A story about a weather plane gone missing hardly qualified as front-page news.

Two days later, Khrushchev appeared before the annual meeting of the Supreme Soviet, the USSR's governing body. "Comrade Deputies," he shouted, "I must report to you on aggressive actions against the Soviet Union in the past few weeks by the United States of America." He then revealed that Soviet forces had shot down the American spy plane over Russian territory.

The audience broke into applause, with yells of "Shame to the aggressor! Shame to the aggressor!"

On May 6, Eisenhower and his advisers doubled down on their cover story, as reporters in Washington began asking questions about Khrushchev's accusations. Bissell and his engineers had taken care to leave no trace of the CIA's involvement in the flight. And, besides, they assumed that Powers died in the crash—taking with him the only evidence of the U-2 flight's real mission.

On May 7, Khrushchev once again climbed the podium at the meeting of the Supreme Soviet.

"Comrades," he began, "I must let you in on a secret." Khrushchev had masterfully withheld the news until now, expecting that the United States would be caught out in a lie.

"When I made my report two days ago," he continued, "I deliberately refrained from mentioning that we have the remains of the plane—and we also have the pilot, who is quite alive and kicking!"

As his speech reached a crescendo, Khrushchev played up the theater of the moment to the hilt. With a sudden flourish, he produced the poisoned pin Powers had removed from the silver dollar.

"He was to jab himself with this poison pin,"

Khrushchev proclaimed, "which would have killed him instantly. What barbarism! Here it is, the latest achievement of American technology for killing their own people!"

As Eisenhower predicted, the U-2 scandal exploded the new relationship between the United States and the Soviet Union. International headlines took aim at the United States, with one London newspaper taunting that "the Americans have made fools of themselves."

Khrushchev stormed out of the Paris nuclear summit only a day after it began. "I had thought the president sincerely wanted to change his policies and improve relations," he complained, adding, "Now, thanks to the U-2, the honeymoon was over."

★ ★ ★

Out of sight, Francis Gary Powers languished in a small cell measuring eight by fifteen feet, deep inside Lubyanka Prison in central Moscow. "It seemed designed to be as uncomfortable as possible, and it was," he recalled.

The KGB interrogated Powers for sixty-one days straight. "No one knew where I was," Powers recalled thinking. "Quite possibly they presumed me dead. There was nothing anyone could do to help me."

The KGB pressed Powers about every detail of his mission, from the technical capabilities of the U-2 to the altitude of his flight and the identities of his fellow pilots.

Under immense pressure, Powers managed to keep steady, gauging his answers carefully and burying his most important secrets deep inside. He aimed to tell the truth, selectively, while subjected to a seemingly endless barrage of questions:

What is your unit called?
Detachment 10-10.

Where is it based?
Incirlik.

Where is Incirlik?
Adana, Turkey.

How many U-2s are there at Incirlik?
Four or five.

How many U-2 pilots are stationed there?
Seven.

What are their names?
I'm not going to tell you that.

We know them anyway, so you might as well tell us.
Fine, if you already know them, then there's no reason for me to tell you.

And so it continued, day after day. "Despite all their tricks," he remembered, "I had succeeded in keeping from them the most important things I knew." Powers held firm until the interrogations finally came to an end.

★ ★ ★

After months in the KGB prison, including seventy days in solitary confinement, Powers learned that the Soviet government intended to put him on trial for espionage. If convicted, he could be sentenced to death.

Not until the day he walked into the courtroom did Powers comprehend that his trial would be, in his words, "a show."

Nearly a thousand spectators crowded into the galleries. Television cameras filmed everything. From a distance, he spotted his wife, Barbara, and his parents, who had been granted travel visas from the Soviet government in order to attend the trial. "Neither of my parents had ever been outside the United States before," Powers remarked. "They looked so alone, so alien in the strange land, that I choked up."

It soon became clear that the Soviets meant to use Powers as a pawn in a campaign to embarrass the United States. "I realized that the trial would not be the *USSR v. Francis Gary Powers*, but the *USSR v. the US*, and incidentally, Francis Gary Powers." If that was the case, he wasn't going to play along.

Powers's calm demeanor left a strong impression on

Francis Gary Powers on the stand during his trial for espionage.
Getty Images

the spectators. A British reporter covering the trial marveled at "this crew-cut, diffident, simple, rather polite man, surrounded by the entire apparatus of Soviet law."

On the US home front, however, some Americans expressed doubts about Powers's loyalty. Rumors swirled that he might be a double agent, or that he planned to defect to the USSR after the trial.

Many US newspapers questioned whether Powers should be considered a traitor. Had he cooperated with the KGB interrogators, as many suspected? Had he revealed American secrets to the Soviets? And if he had a poisoned pin, wouldn't it have been braver of him to use it? The prominent intellectual Robert Maynard Hutchins highlighted "the difference in behavior of Airman Powers and of Nathan Hale" (the American Revolutionary hero who reportedly declared, "I only regret that I have but one life to lose for my country"). Powers had simply wanted to stay alive and make it home; now his own countrymen were chiding him for not committing suicide.

The verdict came down on Friday, August 19: As his family looked on, the court found Francis Gary Powers guilty of "criminal acts" against the Soviet people and sentenced him to ten years in prison. "Only as I was being led from the courtroom did the full impact of the sentence hit me," Powers later wrote. He was briefly led into a private room, where his wife and parents were waiting, surrounded by guards. "Seeing them," he said, "I broke down and cried. They were all crying too."

On September 9, 1960, Powers passed through the gates of Vladimir Central Prison, 150 miles east of Moscow. High walls topped with searchlights enclosed his cell block; guards with machine guns patrolled the perimeter. Powers's new prison cell, which he shared with a political prisoner from Latvia, was even smaller than his previous one. "Supper the first night," he recalled, "consisted of one item—boiled potatoes."

★ ★ ★

Powers faded from public view, but what he could not know is that for the next two years, the CIA maneuvered in secret to bring its man home.

In 1962, CIA officials learned that the Soviets might be willing to exchange Powers for a senior KGB agent, Colonel Rudolf Abel, who was then languishing in a US federal prison in Georgia. Several years earlier, the US government had convicted Abel of running a network of Soviet spies in the United States. During a gripping, highly publicized trial, Abel fought the government's espionage charges with the help of James Donovan, a court-appointed lawyer. Donovan faced heated public criticism for defending a Soviet spy. But he insisted on Abel's right to a fair trial and mounted a deft—though unsuccessful—defense.

After the U-2 incident, CIA officials approached Donovan to act as an unofficial broker in a spy trade of Abel for Powers.

For four days in February 1962, Donovan shuttled between West Berlin and East Berlin, carrying messages between the two sides and carefully negotiating the terms of release. Each evening, when Donovan arrived back in West Berlin, he would dial a phone number and announce, "Jim D. is back." His CIA contact would then meet him at the Berlin Hilton, where they would debrief the day's events. A report was then wired directly to the White House.

On the frigid morning of February 9, 1962, Donovan stood at one end of the Glienicke Bridge in West Berlin, staring across at the VoPos guarding the entrance to the Eastern sector. He had brought along one of Powers's colleagues from the U-2 program, David Murphy, to confirm Powers's identity.

Under the carefully planned handoff, the two spies would be let go at precisely the same moment. At the opposite end of the bridge, Francis Gary Powers was shackled to two East German guards and accompanied by a Soviet colonel. Before the trade, Murphy was allowed to cross over to meet briefly with Powers.

"His was the first familiar face I had seen in a very long time," Powers recalled.

Under instructions from the CIA, Murphy asked a question that only Powers could know the answer to: "What was the name of your high-school football coach?" (The CIA had discovered that information in Powers's personnel files.) The trouble was, under the stress of the moment, Powers couldn't remember. Instead, he quickly rattled off the names of his mother, his wife, and even his dog. That clinched it.

"You're Francis Gary Powers," Murphy said.

"Powers and Abel moved forward with their bags and crossed the center line," Donovan recalled. They passed one another without speaking, each man proceeding to the opposite end of the bridge.

One year and nine months after his U-2 spy plane was shot down by the Soviets, the pilot-spy Francis Gary Powers crossed into West Berlin, a free man.

The SM-65 Atlas, the United States' first ICBM, being launched in 1957.

United States Air Force

6

MISSILES

The Soviet colonel had seen the American students before. A few days earlier, he had sat behind them on the train from Kiev to Moscow; he would have approached them then, but they were being watched by a "minder," or an agent assigned by the KGB. It was much too dangerous: The KGB kept all foreigners in the Soviet Union under close surveillance. He vowed to find them once again on the streets of the capital city, and next time, he would be ready.

Now, late at night in the heart of Moscow, on August 12, 1960, he spied them once again. The two young men crossed Red Square, just a few steps from the Kremlin and the majestic Saint Basil's Orthodox Cathedral...and only a short walk from the headquarters of the KGB, in Lubyanka Prison. They appeared to be totally unguarded. The colonel had to make his move.

As they crossed Moskvoretsky Bridge, spanning the Moskva River, the Russian man joined them, striking up a conversation in shaky English. Though surprised, Eldon Ray Cox and Henry Lee Cobb found the man unthreatening. The Russian was well dressed, his red hair swept back; he appeared to be in his forties.

"I have tried to get in touch with other Americans," he said in heavily accented English. Then he got to the point. "I have some information which I wish to give directly to the American embassy," he said.

He handed the students a thick envelope, begging them to take it immediately to the US embassy in Moscow, which was not far away. The Russian man seemed desperate for help. "I cannot go to the American embassy myself," he told them.

When Cox and Cobb seemed to grow skeptical, the Russian man launched into a story that grabbed their attention. He knew things—secret information from high-level sources—about Francis Gary Powers and the U-2 incident. He told them, for example, that the U-2 plane had not been shot down by a single missile, as Khrushchev had announced publicly, but by fourteen rockets, and by MiG fighter jets as well.

But their intriguing encounter was cut short. The Russian spotted a police officer and, as quickly as he appeared, disappeared into the night, leaving the two Americans with the envelope, uncertain what to do. Cobb was doubtful and feared they were being drawn into a trap. Cox, however, sensed that the unusual man might be telling the truth. He found a taxi and took it the short distance to the American embassy.

Cox delivered the envelope to the security officer on duty at the embassy, who warned him that the embassy "gets a lot of stuff like this from tourists." Cox went home to bed, confused and disappointed, not knowing what to think about the mysterious Russian man.

★ ★ ★

Several hours later, at two AM, a small group of American officials gathered at a table inside a clear plastic box, enclosed with double walls of plexiglass and suspended from wires in a secure room inside the embassy. Eight years earlier, American agents had discovered "bugs," or tiny listening devices, embedded inside the Great Seal of the United States in the US ambassador's office. Ever since then, they feared—correctly—that the Soviets would go to great lengths to eavesdrop on conversations inside the embassy. Only the ten-by-six-foot chamber known as "the bubble" offered total protection from prying KGB ears.

The envelope's contents lay across the table. One of the American officials, a Russian speaker, translated a letter typed in Cyrillic script for the other men present:

> *My dear Sir!*
> *I request that you pass the following to the*
> *authorities in the United States of America.*
> *It is your good friend who is turning to*
> *you, a friend who has already become your*
> *soldier-warrior for the cause of Truth, for the*
> *ideals of a truly free world and of Democracy for*
> *Mankind . . .*

The writer went on to describe, in precise terms that only a spy would understand, procedures for a dead drop in Moscow. He wanted the CIA to pass him instructions for how to give them a large package, containing information on every known missile or rocket inside the Soviet Union.

The Russian offered a second document as proof of his genuine intentions. It included a list of the names of sixty Soviet secret agents, recently graduated from spy training, who would soon be posted to assignments overseas.

And in a final, tantalizing clue, the Russian included a photograph of three men at a party. On the left was an American colonel; on the right, another soldier looked away, his face obscured; and in the middle stood a Soviet officer, whose face had been cut out of the photograph. Above his head, someone had written the words *I am*.

The photograph passed to the US embassy in Moscow by Oleg Penkovsky, as a means of verifying his identity. The words *I am* are written on the forehead of the man (Penkovsky) whose face is cut out of the image.

Central Intelligence Agency Historical Collections

★ ★ ★

Several days later and thousands of miles away, at CIA headquarters in Washington, DC, experts pored over the letters and debated their authenticity. A small army of agents tracked down every name the Russian man had handed over: They were all genuine.

George Kisevalter, a CIA agent who had worked in the Soviet bloc, managed to determine the Russian man's identity from clues in the doctored photograph. Their new informant, the CIA learned, was Oleg Penkovsky, a colonel in the Glavnoe Razvedyvatelnoe Upravlenie (GRU), the Soviet military's main espionage arm. Further research revealed that Penkovsky, as an intelligence officer, had cozied up to some of the highest-ranking members of the Soviet military. And he likely had access to the intelligence the United States desired most: information about the USSR's nuclear missile program.

Kisevalter had no doubts that Penkovsky was the kind of spy the CIA desperately needed. "After all," Kisevalter remarked, "how could anyone present the identities of sixty individuals posted worldwide—all high-ranking, all future placements, all strategic intelligence officers—without going too far?...One does not give away what Penkovsky did as a ploy."

The CIA had never come close to anyone of Penkovsky's stature, or with such potential access to vital secrets.

★ ★ ★

By the time Penkovsky passed his letter to the American students, the American spy agency had been almost totally shut out of the Soviet Union. U-2 flights had stopped over Russia following the Francis Gary Powers incident. The KGB, which guarded the USSR's borders and kept watch over foreigners and Soviet citizens alike, was on high alert. The CIA had few contacts inside the Iron Curtain and even fewer active agents.

Khrushchev's public speeches only made matters worse; he taunted the United States, saying that Russia was "turning out missiles like sausages!" The new American president, John F. Kennedy, refused to be bullied, demanding hard intelligence about the Soviet Union's military capabilities. From the early days of his administration, Kennedy leaned hard on America's spies. "If I need some material fast or an idea fast," Kennedy said, "CIA is the place I have to go."

More than ever, the CIA needed Penkovsky's secrets.

★ ★ ★

There was just one problem. In 1960, the CIA was totally unprepared to "run" an informant in the capital city of its mortal enemy. Not only did the Agency lack a stable of agents who could set up such a delicate operation, but Kisevalter and his associates were not even certain how to get in touch with Penkovsky without exposing him to the KGB.

A new era of espionage was on the horizon. The CIA finally had to learn how to delve into the heart of the Soviet Union itself.

For the moment, though, the chances of succeeding seemed bleak.

At one point, lacking a better plan, the CIA considered signaling to Penkovsky simply to toss the package over the wall of the US embassy as he walked by. (The US ambassador, Llewellyn Thompson, vetoed the idea.) Later, the Agency sent an inexperienced undercover agent, codenamed COMPASS, to pose as a janitor at a residence hall for American embassy staff in Moscow. COMPASS spoke Russian poorly and spent much of his time drinking heavily. After two months of trying, COMPASS never once managed to contact Penkovsky.

"My God, we don't have an operation here," George Kisevalter fretted, "we have a disaster in the making."

★ ★ ★

Fortunately, Penkovsky proved more adept than the Americans at finding a way to communicate with the West. His official "cover" was as a scientific adviser, assigned to organize trips abroad for Soviet technical experts. Desperate to unload his stolen cache of documents, he approached a British businessman in Moscow named Greville Wynne, urging him to take a message to the British embassy. In a stroke of coincidence and good luck, Wynne himself was a onetime spy for Great Britain; he agreed to help, and soon the two men were scheming to organize a meeting in London with representatives from the CIA and MI6.

On the night of April 20, 1961, Oleg Penkovsky slipped away from a delegation of Soviet scientists visiting London. In the same hotel where they were staying, four Western spies, two each from England and the United States, waited to interview the man who had risked his career and his life to reveal some of the Soviet Union's innermost secrets.

As Wynne led him to the room, Penkovsky was gleeful: "I can't believe it, Greville. I just can't believe it." He was ready to cross over, to give everything he could to his new allies in the West.

At that first meeting, the CIA and MI6 learned a great deal about the man they code-named HERO. Unlike George Blake, Penkovsky's grudge against the system that raised him was almost entirely personal.

Oleg's father had been a White Russian, part of the anticommunist movement that fought against the Bolsheviks—the Communists—during the Russian Revolution. Though Penkovsky barely knew his father, and was a committed Communist, suspicion trailed him his whole life. He was passed over for promotions. The perks that came with friends high up in the Communist Party hierarchy never materialized.

By 1960, Oleg Penkovsky had had enough of the Soviet system. He agreed to spy for the West in exchange for money, and for a promise—after two years of passing classified documents to the CIA and MI6—that he and his family would be evacuated to England or America. In a written contract to spy for the CIA and MI6, Penkovsky affirmed that "henceforth I consider myself to be a soldier of the free world fighting for the cause of humanity as a whole and for the freeing from tyrannical rule of the people of my homeland Russia."

He proved his worth as a spy almost immediately, with detailed descriptions of Russia's latest missile systems, the location of missile batteries in Eastern Europe, and technical details about missile launching pads and fuel supplies. Penkovsky also gave the CIA and MI6 a wealth of information about the Soviet leadership, including both rumors and concrete information about political squabbles inside the Kremlin and the Soviet military hierarchy.

Penkovsky's CIA handlers deemed his material so valuable that they decided to protect his identity—from possible moles or potential leaks—with an extra layer of secrecy. The Russian was given two separate code names inside the Agency: IRONBARK, for the military information he provided, and CHICKADEE, for his political espionage. That way, even inside the CIA, it would appear as if Penkovsky's material were coming from different sources, making it more difficult to trace it back to him.

★ ★ ★

Meeting with Penkovsky outside the Soviet Union gave the CIA and MI6 the advantage of working on their own turf. In London and Paris in the ensuing months, they could keep their eyes open for KGB trails and interview the Russian spy at length.

But they needed to find a way to exchange information with Penkovsky in Moscow—a city where nearly every foreign agent was known to the KGB, and every wall, office, and apartment was riddled with bugs.

The solution, in the words of one writer, was "a fit of intelligence lunacy." Penkovsky's unlikely contact, and the key to the success of HERO's operation, was Janet Chisholm, the thirty-two-year-old wife of an official in the

Janet Chisholm and her three children, seated on a bench in a park in Moscow.

Courtesy of Jane Chisholm

British embassy—along with her three young children, two boys and a girl.

On July 2, 1961, Penkovsky entered a park near Tsvetnoy Boulevard in Moscow. It was a typical day in the park in the Russian capital. Children played while parents and elderly retirees watched from their benches. Near the entrances, vendors sold treats from small kiosks.

He had studied the woman's photograph; she was known to him only as ANNA. And now she was sitting not far away, with a baby carriage at her side and three blond children playing close to her. He hesitated, worrying about all of the people nearby. But then he approached, casually greeting her and offering the children a small box of multicolored vitamin C tablets (a common Russian treat during the long winters, when fruits and vegetables were scarce), a plan he had gone over many times with his case officers.

Janet smiled and dropped the box in her baby carriage, thanking him. She then reached in, pulled out an identical decoy box filled with real vitamin tablets, and offered some to her children, who accepted eagerly. The box Penkovsky handed Chisholm lay hidden in the carriage. A short while later, he moved on, leaving them behind.

Inside Penkovsky's box were seven rolls of Minox film and two documents marked ESPECIALLY IMPORTANT AND URGENT, the latter describing the recent deployment of Soviet missile batteries in East Germany.

Between October 1961 and January 1962, Penkovsky

and Chisholm met thirteen times in public places in Moscow. HERO handed over to ANNA undeveloped film containing thousands of images of Soviet documents—so many, at times, that his CIA contacts thought it might be too good to be true. The Agency had to employ thirty translators just to process all the information flowing in.

The CIA had broken through the wall of secrecy around the Soviet Union at last. Penkovsky, the most productive spy ever to work for the Americans, was living up to his code name.

★ ★ ★

In the fall of 1962, events halfway across the globe would reveal the value of HERO's espionage.

Just ninety miles off the coast of Florida, the island nation of Cuba was fast becoming a flash point in the global Cold War.

In 1959, a rebel force led by Fidel Castro had overthrown the Cuban dictator Fulgencio Batista, an authoritarian leader supported by the United States and by the many American companies doing business on the island. Castro promised a more equitable society based on communist principles. He even went so far as to "nationalize" property and factories owned by Americans, repossessing them for the benefit of the Cuban people.

President Eisenhower, for his part, was determined not to let communism get a foothold a mere ninety miles from Florida. He placed an economic embargo on Cuba, one that prevented any US citizen or company from doing business on the island. Behind the scenes, Eisenhower set into motion a secret plan, dubbed Operation Mongoose, to discredit Castro. John F. Kennedy inherited the scheme when he was inaugurated as president in January 1961.

Bill Harvey, now home after nearly a decade in Berlin, was assigned to lead Operation Mongoose. Among other plots, Harvey attempted to damage Castro's public image by adding chemicals to his cigars that would have made him seem confused and incoherent. Another sought to add special salts to his shoe lining to make his beard fall out.

Castro's hold on Cuba only grew stronger.

Several months into his new presidency, John F. Kennedy approved an attempted invasion of the island. On April 17, 1961, supported by the CIA and by planes flown by American pilots, a force of 1,400 Cuban exiles opposed to Castro landed at the Bay of Pigs. The Cubans, tipped off by informants, were waiting for them.

The carefully planned operation quickly turned to disaster. The Cubans slaughtered 200 invaders in the ensuing battle and took 1,200 prisoner. Castro oversaw the defense of the Bay of Pigs personally, and, far from threatening his hold on Cuba, the botched invasion helped consolidate his power. It was a humiliating defeat for the young and untested US president.

At a superpower summit in Berlin that summer, Khrushchev bullied Kennedy, whom he believed to be weak, inexperienced, and indecisive. "Kennedy is a boy in small pants," Khrushchev said.

His personal impressions of the new American president may well have led the Soviet leader into making a bold and risky move with the Soviets' newest ally, Fidel Castro.

Under Khrushchev's aggressive leadership, communism was starting to spread around the globe. He was willing to spend Russian rubles, and sell Soviet arms, to make allies among the world's developing nations. Khrushchev viewed a new alliance with Cuba as a chance to extend Soviet influence to America's backyard; Fidel Castro welcomed the chance to bolster his defenses against his aggressive American neighbor.

Khrushchev also had a deeper motive for wanting to make friends with Castro. The United States had installed Jupiter medium-range missiles, topped with nuclear warheads, along the Turkish-Russian border, putting them within easy range of Moscow. With only a small battery of ICBMs powerful enough to reach the United States, and none of them completely reliable, Khrushchev felt that he needed a much bigger bargaining chip with Kennedy.

Cuba could provide him with a convenient launching pad for his missiles.

In the summer and fall of 1962, Khrushchev made his move. Under the cloak of extreme secrecy, Soviet merchant ships began ferrying R-12 medium-range nuclear missile parts, launchers, and technicians to Cuba. The disassembled missiles were lashed to the decks of cargo ships—including, ironically, many American-made vessels that had been given to the Soviet Union during World War II, when the two nations were allies.

While American officials knew that Soviet troops had already landed on Cuba to help Castro's government, they had no idea that Khrushchev was quietly assembling a nuclear arsenal on the Caribbean island.

By the time aerial photographs taken by U-2 spy planes picked up suspicious behavior on Cuba, it was much too late.

At this key moment, as analysts scrutinized the U-2 photographs of Soviet bases in Cuba, one of the secret documents handed over by Penkovsky earlier that year took on a special significance.

Penkovsky had gotten his hands on a technical manual describing the *same* R-12 missiles that the CIA had detected in Cuba. Using Penkovsky's data as a guide, CIA officials came to a shocking conclusion: The Soviet nuclear missiles on Cuba were close to being fully operational. And, "far from being defensive and of short range," one analysis concluded, "the missiles were armed with 3,000-pound nuclear warheads and range of some 1,000 nautical miles, and were more than capable of reaching Washington, DC, and New York City."

As both the president's brother and his attorney general—the top law-enforcement officer in the United States—Robert F. ("Bobby") Kennedy had a front-row seat to what happened next.

"On Tuesday morning, October 16, 1962, shortly after 9:00," Bobby recalled, "President Kennedy called and asked me to come to the White House. He said only that we were facing great trouble."

The thirteen days that followed became known in the United States as the "Cuban Missile Crisis" and in the Soviet Union as the "Caribbean Crisis." What began as a tense standoff between the two superpowers now threatened to spiral into an actual nuclear conflict.

At seven PM on October 22, 1962, President Kennedy went on television to explain the crisis to the American people. In what one historian has called the "scariest presidential address in all of US history," Kennedy announced to the American people—and to Khrushchev himself—that America and the Soviet Union were on a collision course:

This government, as promised, has maintained the closest surveillance of the Soviet military buildup on the island of

Cuba. Within the past week, unmistakable evidence has
established the fact that a series of offensive missile
sites is now in preparation on that imprisoned island. The
purpose of these bases can be none other than to provide
a nuclear strike capability against the Western Hemisphere.

On the basis of the intelligence Penkovsky provided,
Kennedy and his aides realized that there was only a
small window in which to act, before Khrushchev's missiles became fully operational. If they were going to force
the Soviet leader to back down, now was the time. The
president immediately announced a "quarantine" of Cuba,
enforced by US Navy ships, and declared, "We will not
prematurely or unnecessarily risk the costs of worldwide
nuclear war in which even the fruits of victory would be
ashes in our mouth—but neither will we shrink from that
risk at any time it must be faced."

What the American and Russian public *didn't* know
was more terrifying still.

Several times during the missile crisis, accidents or
misunderstandings threatened to trigger a sudden nuclear
incident. For example, four Russian submarines prowled
the waters near Cuba, each one carrying a torpedo loaded
with a nuclear weapon. At one point, the commander
of one of the subs feared, incorrectly, that he was under
attack from an American ship on the surface. He ordered

his torpedo into its tube and was only seconds from firing it when he called off the launch.

Similarly, nearly forty years later, researchers discovered that the Soviets had moved short-range nuclear cruise missiles into striking distance of the US military base in Guantánamo Bay. Known as "front-line winged rockets," each of these missiles contained a warhead equal in power to the atomic bomb dropped on Hiroshima. Had Kennedy ordered an invasion of the island—a strategy many of his advisers were clamoring for—the Soviet commanders on Cuba had orders to launch the weapons, which would have obliterated the base.

These and other close calls brought the United States and USSR to within hours of mutual destruction. A single mistake or error of judgment could easily have triggered a chain reaction that would certainly have led to the deaths of millions of people around the globe. "It was just the most devastating event in world history...*that somehow didn't happen*," according to the historian Martin Sherwin.

By the end of the week, with his forces in Cuba encircled by American ships and aircraft, Khrushchev realized that his gamble to place Soviet missiles at America's doorstep had failed. In a letter to Kennedy, hand-delivered to the US embassy in Moscow on Friday, October 26 (which took many hours to translate and transmit via Teletype to

Washington), the Soviet premier indicated a willingness to bring his missiles home.

Kennedy's ability to outmaneuver Khrushchev, and to assess the threat at America's doorstep, depended on the flow of secret intelligence passed to Janet Chisholm in a Moscow park.

"For that brief and critical moment in time," one study of the Cuban Missile Crisis concluded, "history turned on the material provided by one man, Oleg Penkovsky."

The Cuban Missile Crisis had ended.

★ ★ ★

For the CIA, unexpected news from Moscow cut short celebrations over the end of the standoff with the USSR.

On November 2, 1962, an encrypted message arrived at the secure communications center deep inside the newly constructed CIA headquarters on an enormous campus in Langley, Virginia, housing thousands of employees. The message was then hand-delivered to the offices of the Soviet Russia (SR) division, which could be accessed only by CIA staff with special clearance. (Other, less sensitive messages traveled via a pneumatic tube system that could reach everywhere within the 1.4 million–square-foot building.)

Behind the closed and guarded doors of the SR offices, an SR officer deciphered the message by hand, using a one-time pad. Once the message was converted to plaintext, the officer carried it by hand to the SR division chief, who brought it to his superior, who in turn handed it personally to the director of Central Intelligence, or DCI. Only a small circle of CIA personnel had access to the message, but the information it carried had terrifying implications for the entire spy agency.

Richard Jacob, a young CIA officer in Moscow, had been arrested and deported from the Soviet Union. Jacob was caught while "clearing" a dead drop, in the form of a matchbook hidden behind a radiator, in the hallway of an apartment building. The implications of this news were clear to all who read it. Jacob was HERO's CIA handler. The KGB had found Penkovsky.

A little more than five weeks later, the official Soviet newspaper, *Pravda*, made public the arrest of Colonel Oleg Penkovsky. On May 7, 1963, Penkovsky appeared in a Moscow courtroom before the same judge that Francis Gary Powers had faced several years earlier. The verdict came swiftly, with the Soviet judge declaring Penkovsky "guilty of treason to the Motherland."

George Kisevalter and his CIA colleagues could only watch helplessly as Penkovsky's sentence was handed down: death by firing squad. In a last-ditch effort, they hatched a plan to appeal directly to Penkovsky's bosses in the GRU—their sworn enemies—to plead for his life. Kisevalter and another agent drafted a letter to be sent through secret channels in Europe.

"This proposition may come as something of a surprise to you," they wrote, "and you may at first consider it outrageous and impossible. However, we feel it is our duty to take whatever steps and actions may be necessary to protect the life and freedom of Oleg Penkovsky. We have a tremendous obligation to this brave man."

But the letter was never sent. In the heat of the aftermath of the Cuban Missile Crisis, Kisevalter was told bluntly that the CIA "does not communicate with an enemy intelligence service." He had been overruled.

Less than a week later, the Soviet government announced that Oleg Penkovsky had been executed.

★ ★ ★

The CIA attempted to retaliate against the KGB by publishing a book titled *The Penkovsky Papers*, which included reams of new evidence of the Soviets' spying methods in the West, exposing their secrets for all to read.

But inside the walls of the CIA, the spymasters absorbed hard lessons. After Penkovsky's arrest and execution, the CIA learned that his capture was no mere fluke: KGB counterespionage teams had conducted a massive surveillance operation over several months, setting up three separate observation posts near HERO's apartment. One was located in the apartment directly above him. A KGB technical crew drilled a pinhole into the ceiling of his living room and photographed him in action.

When Penkovsky went to trial, the KGB had assembled an airtight case, complete with pictures of him working with stolen military files.

Penkovsky's death did more than shut off the stream of Soviet secrets HERO had provided to the CIA. It was the end, for a long time, of the CIA's confidence in its ability to infiltrate the main enemy. Fearing more losses of precious assets, the CIA canceled operations. Agents were ordered to stand down. Moscow, the CIA concluded, was off-limits. Nearly a decade would pass before the United States regained the know-how or the will to launch espionage operations on Russian soil.

A new generation of agents would have to come on the scene, more than a decade later, before the United States was ready to make its next move against the KGB.

Soviet soldiers guarding the Lenin Mausoleum in Moscow, 1989.

Zuma Press

STALEMATE

Marti Peterson's Soviet driver's license in 1975.

Courtesy of Martha D. Peterson

7

MOSCOW RULES

The telephone in Marti Peterson's hotel room rang twice during the night. Both times, no one was on the line when she picked up. From her training, Marti knew that this might be an old KGB trick—keeping foreigners in Moscow off balance, sleep deprived, and aware of being watched.

In the hallway outside, an old woman called a *dezhurnaya*, or "hall dragon," stood guard over all the room keys, which hung on hooks behind her desk.

Marti's plane had touched down at Moscow's Sheremet-yevo Airport the previous evening. Though it was only November, snow blanketed the capital, and temperatures were dropping fast as the long Russian winter set in. This would be a tough posting for any young CIA officer, let alone the first female field agent ever sent to spy against the Soviet Union.

For more than a decade following Penkovsky's arrest, Moscow had been a virtual no-go zone for CIA operations.

Leonid Brezhnev, who succeeded Khrushchev as Soviet leader in 1964, had given the KGB nearly unlimited power over Soviet society. The KGB's Fifth Directorate policed anyone who dared criticize the system. Some dissidents (as they were known outside of the USSR) were labeled insane and shut away in mental institutions; the KGB summarily executed others. Writers and intellectuals, such as the world-famous novelist Aleksandr Solzhenitsyn, whose books depicted life in Soviet prison camps or gulags, were lucky by comparison—he merely found himself permanently ejected from his homeland in 1974. To many Soviet citizens, life itself seemed frozen in place.

When Marti Peterson arrived in Russia, her fellow agents at the CIA's Moscow station were struggling to shake off a long season of hibernation. Following HERO's arrest, they had stopped recruiting Soviet informers under orders from James Jesus Angleton, the secretive and paranoid CIA chief of counterintelligence. His outlook infected the entire CIA, making it a place where no one could be trusted, and where potential Soviet recruits were assumed to be double agents sent by the KGB.

CIA director William Colby finally forced Angleton to resign in 1974. That same year, CIA operatives made contact with a senior official in the Soviet Foreign Ministry who was stationed at the Russian embassy in Bogotá, Colombia.

Aleksandr Ogorodnik was smart, handsome, and ready to trade secrets for American money. Like many Soviet diplomats, he enjoyed perks that average citizens in the USSR could scarcely hope for, including new cars, restaurant meals, and stylish clothing. Though married, Ogorodnik also carried on a secret love affair with a Colombian woman—who was pregnant with his child.

But there was more to Ogorodnik than a desire for quick cash or a need to untangle his complicated personal life. According to Marti Peterson, after he had been recruited, Ogorodnik "felt more in control over his life than he ever had. He no longer had to follow the path laid out by his father and the Soviet system." Ogorodnik was the ideal informant. The CIA code-named him TRIGON.

The CIA knew that TRIGON could get access to secret Soviet documents inside the embassy. The challenge was, how to make copies when the documents were constantly under guard?

George Saxe, a veteran CIA case officer, flew down to Bogotá to train TRIGON himself. Before he made contact with the Russian, however, Saxe had to learn how to handle something much more delicate: the T-50 subminiature camera, a tiny device fitted inside a brand-name pen.

A marvel of miniature engineering, the T-50 had a lens only four millimeters wide. Its one-and-a-half-inch case held enough film for fifty exposures. The film itself, loaded into the T-50 by specially trained technicians, was barely wider than the lens—a mere five millimeters.

To take a clear photograph, an agent had to hold the pen exactly eleven inches above a document, using his forearms as a kind of tripod. With practice, Saxe realized that he could cradle the pen gently in his hands while leaning on his elbows, snapping perfect images. To an uninformed observer, Saxe seemed to be reading, innocently.

During clandestine meetings with Saxe in a hotel room in Bogotá, TRIGON mastered the T-50 in a matter of weeks.

The CIA's Office of Technical Service (OTS) had developed the T-50 in the years following Penkovsky's arrest, with the goal of creating a camera that could be easily hidden or smuggled inside an agent's clothing or personal belongings. That way, the CIA hoped, an agent or informer could steal secrets from inside the heart of the KGB itself, an unheard-of feat (and one that even Penkovsky, who worked for the Soviet military intelligence wing, had never achieved).

"The craftsmanship and the technology that went into making the lens assembly was something that may never be repeated," Saxe later commented.

Saxe was one of a new generation of CIA operatives who pushed hard to get more aggressive in recruiting Soviet informers. With Angleton gone, the Operations Directorate maneuvered for new opportunities to penetrate deep into the heart of Brezhnev's secretive and rigid government.

When news came that TRIGON had received a transfer back to Moscow, they had their chance.

In Ogorodnik's suitcase on his flight back to Moscow in 1975, the CIA hid a small cache of spy gear, including a microdot (printed text that was shrunken down to a one-millimeter-wide dot) containing information about when and where the Agency would contact him next.

The CIA's Moscow station was about to come alive again.

★ ★ ★

During the day, Marti Peterson held a regular job in the US embassy, working alongside other low-level office workers, most of them Russians (and some of them, she assumed, informers for the KGB). But at night, her real assignment took over. The CIA's Moscow station was a windowless office—a "box," she called it, because the space was so cramped. It was hidden deep inside the embassy walls and could be entered only through an unmarked door sealed with a cipher lock. Within the office, a team of CIA operatives gathered at all hours around small desks, surrounded by maps of Moscow and photographs of potential meeting places and drop sites.

Marti had taken many of these photographs herself. As it turned out, being the Agency's first female officer in Moscow had its advantages: The KGB never caught on to her real position in the CIA. The Russians, accustomed to the gender discrimination in the CIA's ranks (and perhaps blinded by their own beliefs about the proper role of women), simply never imagined that a young woman might be an American spy.

KGB surveillance teams trailed, photographed, and harassed every known or suspected CIA employee in Moscow. KGB observers bugged CIA agents' phones and cataloged their daily routines. Marti once heard a story "about a bug embedded into the sole of an officer's shoe when he sent them to the local cobbler. So," she added, "no one had shoes resoled in Moscow."

Marti Peterson was the only CIA agent in Moscow who could move freely throughout the city. "I soon discovered I had a significant advantage in casing operational sites by not having surveillance," she remarked. Sometimes she took her Zhiguli, a boxy four-cylinder Russian car, on winding drives through the capital. At other times she walked the streets, eyeing potential drop sites and meeting places.

Wherever she went, Marti carried a Nikon camera. It was a keepsake, the one possession that remained from her previous life with her husband, John, who also worked for the CIA. During the Vietnam War, John and Marti Peterson spent three perilous years together in neighboring Laos, where John trained and advised a guerrilla army to fight the communist insurgency there. He loved photography and always kept the camera strapped over his shoulder.

When John died in a helicopter crash during the Vietnam War, Marti returned to the United States in a state of stunned disbelief. She lived for months on her parents' couch. It was not until a friend suggested that she join the CIA herself that Marti could imagine a path forward. Now she snapped photographs with John's camera wherever she went, creating a visual map of the Russian capital for the CIA.

★ ★ ★

After months of waiting and preparations, the time had come to make contact with TRIGON.

The male agents at the CIA Moscow station handled the first dead drops. TRIGON began supplying rolls of film that were chock-full of highly classified Soviet documents, intelligence that the CIA transmitted directly to the White House. The new spy was a gold mine of Soviet secrets.

During these early months of her Moscow assignment, Marti knew that her fellow CIA agents could not truly accept that the KGB hadn't noticed her. To them, the answer to why she thought she wasn't being tailed was simple: She lacked the experience to pick up on her KGB surveillance team. She reassured herself by recalling some advice from a CIA colleague who had worked for many years under the harsh conditions in Moscow. "He anticipated that I would have to tolerate some strong male egos in Moscow who might doubt I could do the job," she remembered. "He suggested I not let the male case officers' bluster fool me.... He knew I had suffered, had overcome loss, and had pulled myself back up. I felt stronger as I considered his confidence in me."

A veteran agent named Mike came up with a plan to put his fellow (male) agents' doubts to rest. One Saturday morning, Mike and his wife positioned themselves on the second floor of a large Moscow store, overlooking the street. They watched through a large plate-glass window as Marti drove by in her Zhiguli car, according to plan. If a KGB surveillance team were following Marti, Mike would see them.

Mike confirmed it—Marti was clean.

As TRIGON's value as a spy grew, so did Marti's special status as the only CIA agent who had escaped the notice of KGB watchers.

On April 1, 1976, TRIGON parked his car in a designated spot near his mother's house, signaling that he was ready for his next dead drop. The Agency's station chief decided to put Marti on the case.

"I was prepared to make this drop," she told herself. "My mission was imminent."

Marti watched as a CIA technician, toiling away in the cramped embassy office, carefully assembled a dead-drop package designed to look like a beat-up pack of cigarettes. She marveled at the number of items he managed to fit inside: a T-50 subminiature camera, film cassettes, one-time pads (to decode radio communications), and a tightly rolled pack of rubles.

That very night, Marti drove toward the site, watching carefully to make sure she wasn't being followed.

Like all CIA operatives, Marti strapped to her body an SRR-100, a special radio receiver that allowed her to pick up the radio transmissions of KGB surveillance teams that might be tailing her. Listening through an earpiece molded to look like her actual ear, Marti heard nothing. She was under deep cover, moving quietly toward her first dead drop with the CIA's most important Soviet informant.

Marti parked at a subway station, hopped on a train

for a few stops, and then followed a long and winding route on foot. Her many months of learning the maze of Moscow streets alone, unwatched, paid off. When she reached the dead-drop site, she pretended to sneeze and then dropped the pack. She walked away as it landed safely in place, next to a lamppost.

But when Marti came back over an hour later, the cigarette pack was still there. TRIGON had not shown up.

Two-way communication with TRIGON was impossible in the 1970s—the days before cell phones, the Internet, and other forms of digital or remote communication. Marti and her colleagues had no way of knowing what had happened or what was going through TRIGON's mind when he decided not to "clear" the dead drop. Any attempt to approach him directly would put TRIGON, and the operation, at extreme risk. All they could do now was wait, worry, and watch for TRIGON's car to reappear in the parking spot at a future date.

And then, at last, on June 20, 1976, the car appeared once again.

On June 21, Marti prepared for a second attempt. This time, she carried a small container that was camouflaged to look exactly like a wooden log, complete with real bark. As before, it contained messages and equipment for TRIGON, as well as a roll of rubles. This dead-drop container, however, concealed something specially cushioned, and—to Marti—ominous. At TRIGON's request, while he was still in Colombia, the CIA had assembled a second pen, containing a breakable vial of cyanide poison. TRIGON viewed this pen as a kind of insurance policy. He had no intention of being caught, or interrogated, by the KGB.

"I felt sorry as well as fear for him," Marti recalled.

The log also contained a note in Russian, aimed at preventing any unsuspecting Soviet citizen from getting into trouble with the authorities: "If by chance you have found this log and opened it, you should not go any further. Take this roll of money. Throw the log and the rest of its contents into the river, as possessing this will put you in grave danger."

For the second time in her brief CIA career, Marti headed out into the Moscow night.

This time, the dead drop was a success—TRIGON took the supplies Marti had left and replaced them with his own film and messages. Marti returned to the office the next day with the precious package from TRIGON, setting into motion a six-month period of meetings and exchanges that would make Ogorodnik one of the most productive CIA informants of the entire Cold War.

Then, in the winter of 1977, TRIGON's communications took a strange turn. His photographs were blurry, their edges smudged. He repeatedly missed dead drops. Marti, in particular, worried about him. She felt that he was taking huge risks to help the United States and that the stress of his secret life was beginning to show.

In early July, eager to keep up the flow of secret documents, the CIA team decided to send a one-way voice link (OWVL) message to TRIGON, instructing him to make a red mark on a specific street sign as a signal that he would pick up a dead drop from Marti the following day. (OWVL messages were broadcast over open shortwave radio frequencies, with a voice reading coded words that only TRIGON—using his one-time pad—could decipher.)

On the morning of July 15, Marti reported that TRIGON had left his red mark on the sign. She sensed something wrong, however. The mark was too perfect, almost as if someone had stenciled it carefully. But the need to make contact with TRIGON was too important to put off another drop.

That evening, she left work as usual. She went home and changed into casual clothes, put on her SRR-100 radio receiver and earpiece, and slipped a small chunk of asphalt into her purse. The asphalt "rock" concealed rubles, T-50 camera cartridges, emerald jewelry (which TRIGON planned to give to his mother, purchased with his CIA earnings), one-time pads, and other supplies.

The CIA chose a dead-drop site on a railroad bridge over the Moskva River, away from the city center, near a sports stadium. In a previous drop, the CIA provided TRIGON with a map showing the location.

Marti scanned for surveillance confidently; the street running along the railroad tracks seemed deserted. "All

MOSCOW RULES ★ 159

was quiet," she noted. At 10:15 PM, she placed the rock, as planned, in a stone window in the railroad bridge, and pushed it one arm's length from the edge.

Only TRIGON would know where to find it.

As Marti descended the stairs, three men in white shirts appeared from across the road, moving quickly toward her. Trapped in this remote spot, she wasn't sure what to think about their intentions—but they did not seem friendly. "My question was whether I was going to be raped, or mugged, or worse," she recalled thinking.

The men closed in and grabbed her, tearing at the radio receiver under her arm. "They smelled bad," she recalled, "a stale, sweaty, male odor, their bodies pressing on me to restrain me." She shouted, hoping to warn TRIGON in case he was nearby.

A van pulled up and a larger group of men jumped out. "You can't hold me," she shouted. "Let go of me. I'm an American. You must call the embassy. The number is 252-00-11." Remembering her training, Marti delivered a powerful kick to one of her captors.

A man in a dark suit stepped forward, taking charge. Speaking English, he commanded Marti to be quiet, while other men in the group took flash photographs and emptied her purse onto the ground.

The men spoke Russian in front of her and clearly had no idea that she understood the language. They knew where she had parked her car, several subway stops away, and one of the men, to her horror, held up the asphalt rock. No one could have seen her place it; they had to have known about the plan in advance. Had TRIGON been betrayed?

Two men hustled Marti into the van, clinging hard to her wrists. They sped to the back door of Lubyanka Prison. As she passed through, she caught sight of a brass plaque that read: PRESIDIUM, KGB.

Marti Peterson during her filmed interrogation at Lubyanka Prison, with the contents of the dead-drop package laid out on the table.

KGB photograph

The men led Marti into a room bustling with other Russian agents. Her interrogation began quickly, with tape recorders whirring and cameras filming. A Russian official ticked off the charges against her. As she listened, a technician took apart the asphalt rock, placing each bit of spy gear and equipment on the table, one by one.

The KGB alerted an official from the US embassy, who joined Marti at the table. He protested her innocence. As the interrogation unfolded, however, he was no less astonished that Marti Peterson was a CIA spy than the KGB agents assembled around them. She had stayed deep undercover.

At two AM, Marti's ordeal ended as quickly as it had begun. She had been unmasked as a CIA operative, thereby rendering her useless as an undercover agent in the Soviet Union. But Marti privately took some pleasure in imagining the scene in KGB headquarters on Monday morning. "I wonder how many KGB officers lost their jobs," she mused to herself, "when they found no continuous record of what I had done since arriving in Moscow on November 5, 1975."

"You may leave," said the interrogator.

Following accepted protocol for dealing with enemy spies, the Soviets declared Marti persona non grata (PNG) and ordered her to leave the Soviet Union immediately. At nine AM on Monday, July 18, 1977, Marti Peterson boarded a flight to Washington, DC, and left the USSR for good.

Marti could not help but feel that a cloud of suspicion hung over her. Had she done something to put TRIGON at risk? Did her lack of training blind her to KGB surveillance? "I knew that some thought I had become sloppy or had missed surveillance during a critical delivery," she reflected. "It was the mid-1970s, and some thought that they should have sent a man, not a woman." Worse, neither Marti nor anyone in the CIA knew TRI-GON's fate—or if he would ever resurface.

★ ★ ★

On Monday afternoon, not long after arriving—exhausted— in Washington, Marti Peterson was due for a debriefing with Admiral Stansfield Turner, the director of Central Intelligence. The government's top brass wanted to hear directly from Marti about their most precious Russian spy.

During her meeting with Turner, the DCI offered Marti an unusual invitation. The very next day, she stood outside the Oval Office doors, waiting to brief Jimmy Carter, the president of the United States, on the TRIGON case.

Carter was captivated by her story. Marti had brought a duplicate copy of the asphalt rock and offered riveting details of her capture. Zbigniew Brzezinski, the Polish-born national security adviser—and a vocal anticommunist—reached out to shake Marti's hand as she left the Oval Office.

"I greatly admire your courage," he said.

On Wednesday, Marti received a handwritten note from Admiral Turner. It read:

You are the only person who has stood face-to-face with the KGB and the President of the United States all within three days. I admire and congratulate you.

★ ★ ★

Years later, the CIA pieced together what had happened to TRIGON.

Two sleeper agents from communist Czechoslovakia had been living for nearly a decade in the United States, posing as defectors and staunch anticommunists. Karl and Hana Koecher cut dashing figures as an attractive, party-loving couple. Karl obtained his PhD in philosophy from Columbia University—where one of his professors was Zbigniew Brzezinski.

The Koechers moved to Washington in 1975, and Karl landed a job as a translator for the CIA, where he was allowed to listen in on top secret recordings. On one occasion, he was asked to translate Russian reports from a Soviet diplomat being recruited by the CIA in Bogotá, Colombia.

Karl quietly passed this information to his KGB contacts. It was only a matter of time before the KGB homed in on Aleksandr Ogorodnik.

In fact, documents later revealed that the KGB had arrested TRIGON long before Marti's final, fateful dead-drop attempt—which was all a setup to catch his contact. In April 1977, KGB agents intercepted Ogorodnik as he left

his apartment building in Moscow and took him to Lubyanka Prison for interrogation. He was brought to a cell
and stripped to his underwear. At that moment, TRIGON
declared that he would admit everything in writing and
asked for his pen. Before his captors could stop him, he bit
down on the tip of the CIA-designed device, breaking a
vial of cyanide poison. He died instantly.

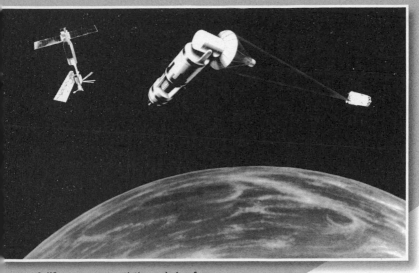

A US government artist's rendering from September 1984 of the Strategic Defense Initiative, which envisioned a network of space-based lasers and other weaponry designed to intercept Soviet ICBMs.

United States Air Force

8

WAR GAMES

O n June 11, 1985, KGB colonel Oleg Gordievsky set his final plan into motion. After years of spying for MI6, the double agent knew that his luck had run out. When, just three weeks earlier, his KGB bosses had recalled him to Moscow from London, Gordievsky feared that he might disappear immediately into the bowels of Lefortovo Prison, the KGB dungeon.

The escape instructions, prepared carefully by his MI6 handlers, had been sealed into the hardcover binding of a book. The spy soaked the book in water to dissolve the glue that held the binding together. When it loosened, he removed a cellophane-wrapped sheet.

As a precaution, he recopied the instructions onto a separate paper, using shorthand that only he would recognize. In case KGB agents searched his apartment, he took the paper to the basement garage of his apartment building in Moscow, crumpled it into a ball, and pushed it carefully into a gap between two bricks in the wall.

Somehow, he was still alive, but they were watching him. Time was not on Oleg Gordievsky's side.

★ ★ ★

Oleg Gordievsky's career as a double agent had landed him right in the middle of one of the most dangerous standoffs of the Cold War—and into scalding-hot water with the KGB.

Only a few years earlier, in 1981, relations between America and the USSR had taken a nosedive. The new president, Ronald Reagan, was a lifelong enemy of communism; in the late 1940s, as a Hollywood actor, Reagan had helped lead the "witch hunts" that sought to root Soviet sympathizers, real or imagined, out of the movie industry. If anything, Reagan's opposition to communism and the Soviet Union had only grown since the McCarthy era, and in 1981 he brought into the White House a new generation of hard-line anticommunists, men and women who believed that the Soviet "menace" must be countered around the world—whether in Poland, Afghanistan, or Nicaragua—by any means.

The president declared détente—the attempt to improve relations between America and Russia—a failure. Calling the Soviet Union an "evil empire," Reagan ordered the largest peacetime military buildup ever. The Pentagon's budget more than doubled from 1981 to 1986, as America added new nuclear missiles, the Trident nuclear submarine, and the B-1 nuclear bomber. Reagan's Strategic Defense Initiative (nicknamed "Star Wars") envisioned a vast network of space satellites armed with lasers, designed to thwart a Soviet missile launch.

In his memoirs, Reagan wrote, "I intended to let the Soviets know that we were going to spend what it took to stay ahead of them in the arms race."

Ronald Reagan's words and actions shocked the Soviets. For the first time since the days of the Cuban Missile Crisis, it seemed to Kremlin officials that America had revived the threat of actual nuclear war. Fearing a first-strike nuclear attack by the United States, the Soviet Union resolved not to let its guard down. In 1981, KGB chairman Yuri Andropov launched Operation RYaN (or Raketno-Yadernoye Napadenie, Russian for "nuclear missile attack"), a global espionage program aimed at sniffing out signs that America was preparing a nuclear launch.

A steady stream of telltale clues fueled the Soviets'

fears. Inside the United States, the KGB maintained high-tech listening stations on the roofs of the Soviet embassy, the Soviet mission to the United Nations in New York, and at consulates in major cities across the country. Technicians could even pick up telephone conversations between US government limousines' car phones and offices in the State Department and the Pentagon.

Agents watched for the movement of missile batteries, the sudden evacuation of military personnel to fallout shelters, and even an increase in collections from American blood banks (a sign that the United States was preparing for mass casualties). Some KGB personnel even tracked when the lights were left on at night at American military bases in Germany. Could longer working hours mean that the enemy was working overtime, preparing for war? their bosses wondered.

By 1983, the surge in superpower hostility had made life in the KGB's London residency even more oppressive than usual. Colonel Oleg Gordievsky grew weary of the intensive countermeasures taken by the security staff. "Inside the Embassy, life was dominated by a terrible paranoia about bugging: often the staff appeared able to think of nothing else," Gordievsky commented. Electric typewriters were forbidden lest they be bugged by MI6. Even manual typewriters had been banned, for fear that eavesdroppers could somehow decipher what was being typed from the sound of the keys. Jamming devices located throughout the offices made constant buzzing noises. Notices on every wall in the residency announced: DON'T SAY NAMES OR DATES OUT LOUD.

Some of Gordievsky's colleagues even wondered if their gardener was an MI6 agent.

Ironically, amid such intense suspicion of the British, no one seemed to take note of the double agent inside the KGB's London residency.

Oleg Gordievsky had spied enthusiastically for MI6 for seven years, having switched sides in 1976, while working at the Soviet embassy in Copenhagen. After transferring to the KGB's London residency, he developed a close personal relationship with his two MI6 handlers, Jack and Joan, with whom he met regularly for clandestine lunchtime meetings at a safe house not far from the Soviet embassy. "Once clear of the Embassy," Gordievsky recalled, "we KGB were free to move around as we liked, without restrictions: we were operational officers, expected to initiate our own contacts."

As a senior KGB official, Gordievsky knew well the penalty for sharing Soviet secrets with the enemy: a long sentence in a prison camp or, more likely, execution by firing squad. Nobody in his circle of friends or family knew the truth about his double role—not even his wife, Leila, let alone his two daughters. "Because Leila had grown up very much a Soviet girl, heavily indoctrinated by Communist propaganda," he said, "I never dared tell her that I was working for the British for fear that she would denounce me." Gordievsky considered himself a devoted family man, but his secrets and lies created an inevitable distance between him and those he loved most.

Gordievsky did not oppose the Soviet system. Rather, he had watched with dismay as his country slid into stagnation in the 1970s. "I saw the queues, the shortages, the filthiness of public lavatories, the bureaucracy, the corruption, the red tape, the rudeness of officials, the impossibility of obtaining redress when one had a complaint," he remembered. "When I saw all this, I felt physically ill.

"Everything was deteriorating," he recalled, "standards of behavior as much as physical conditions. The optimism of the early 1960s under Khrushchev had died away; then, at least, there had been a feeling that although the regime was still Communist, it was going forward. In the 1970s, under Brezhnev, the feeling was not merely of no progress but of retrogression.

"I was living and working on the frontier between the totalitarian world and the West," he observed, "seeing both sides, and constantly angered by the contrast between the two."

Pained by what he saw as his country's decline, Gordievsky believed that his country's only hope for survival was to lose out to the West and to open itself up to democratic ideas. He looked on his work with MI6, to whom he passed thousands of KGB documents, as one small part of this important mission.

But would his work make any difference? he wondered. Ever since Reagan's election, the United States and the Soviet Union had been moving further apart, not closer together. As one of the only people in the world who had access to high-level intelligence reports from both the KGB *and* the CIA (through his close relationship with the Agency's London station), Gordievsky watched with trepidation as the Cold War slid toward open hostility.

And in the fall of 1983, things took a dangerous turn.

On September 1, the pilot of a Soviet interceptor jet launched air-to-air missiles at Korean Air Lines flight 007, which Soviet ground crews had mistaken for a hostile military aircraft. The passenger jet had left Seoul earlier that day, bound for Anchorage, Alaska, and had deviated off course into Soviet airspace. Two hundred sixty-nine people died in the crash. One of them, Larry McDonald, was a sitting US congressman.

The Soviets accused the plane of engaging in espionage and blasted the CIA for committing a "criminal, provocative act." An enraged President Reagan called the downing of Korean Airlines flight 007 "an act of barbarism." The United States responded by banning all commercial Soviet flights from US airspace.

Then, in November of that same year, KGB surveillance

teams detected NATO military maneuvers that appeared to be final preparations for war. One hundred seventy flights transported 19,000 troops from the United States to Western Europe. B-52 bombers were detected moving out of hangars, carrying nuclear weapons. Tanks rolled across West German fields. US military leaders moved to DEFCON (or defense condition) 1, the highest state of alert for its armed forces, which indicated that war might be imminent.

Earlier that year, a top secret KGB report described DEFCON 1 as "when there are obvious indications of preparations to begin military operations. It is considered that war is inevitable and may start at any moment."

On November 5, Gordievsky read a telegram that had arrived from KGB headquarters:

> surprise is the key element in the main adversary's (United States') plans and preparations for war in today's conditions...up to the order to deliver the strike will be of very short duration, possibly 7-10 days.

On November 8 or 9, Gordievsky received a second flash telegram. "The countdown to a nuclear first strike [has] actually begun," it read.

Soviet forces in Eastern Europe, including nuclear missile crews, moved into high alert.

At that moment, Oleg Gordievsky may have been the only Soviet official who knew the truth of what was taking place: America and its NATO allies were launching not an attack but rather a series of realistic military exercises, dubbed Able Archer 83. The maneuvers were simply drills; the nuclear warheads that KGB agents had spied being loaded onto B-52s were dummies.

Neither President Reagan nor the United States' NATO allies intended to attack the USSR. In fact, no one in the White House or NATO headquarters had any inkling of the alarms going off through the corridors of the Kremlin and the Soviet military hierarchy. To America, Able Archer 83 was a mock exercise—neither the first nor the last that it would conduct during the Cold War. To the Soviet leadership, put on the defensive by Reagan's belligerent rhetoric and by the suspicious information collected by Operation RYaN, the maneuvers seemed terrifyingly real.

At this critical moment, Gordievsky managed to persuade his MI6 contacts that the Soviets had misread NATO's intentions. Messages ricocheted through NATO headquarters, the CIA, and the White House. On November 11, the maneuvers halted.

Several months later, CIA director William Casey carried a full report to the president about Soviet attitudes during the crisis, based on the intelligence provided by Gordievsky.

"Do you suppose they really believe that?" the president said to his national security adviser, Robert "Bud" McFarlane.

"I don't see how they could believe that," Reagan mused, "but it's something to think about."

As with the spy Penkovsky before him, the information Gordievsky passed to his handlers, experts believe, may well have defused a global crisis and averted nuclear war.

★ ★ ★

On Thursday, May 17, 1984, what should have been good news sounded to Gordievsky like a death sentence.

The KGB had just promoted him to *rezident* of the KGB's London station, putting him in charge of all spying operations in the British capital. Then, according to Gordievsky, "the thunderbolt struck.

"I was sitting at my desk in the resident's office," he recalled, "when the cipher clerk brought in a telegram. As I read the handwritten message, I felt sweat break out on my back, and for a second or two my vision clouded. Fighting to control myself, I was dreadfully afraid that the clerk must notice how badly shocked I was."

The telegram ordered Gordievsky to return to Moscow to discuss his new job with none other than the chairman of the KGB and the head of the First Chief Directorate. But

Gordievsky was already briefed on his new duties, and he recognized instantly that the meeting was a pretext for something else. All seasoned KGB agents knew that the call to return to Moscow meant serious trouble.

Had someone tipped off the KGB to Gordievsky's double role, or were they just fishing for clues?

Despite his misgivings, he decided to risk the trip.

Gordievsky's suspicions only deepened as he passed through the Moscow airport. The passport officer examined his documents for what seemed like ages. "Then he made a telephone call," Gordievsky recalled. "Watching him through the glass, I could practically see his mind working: he had discovered something wrong." Later he learned that the officer had sent a message to the KGB, confirming that Gordievsky was now on Soviet soil.

Gordievsky arrived at his Moscow apartment a short while later. His door had three locks, but he only ever locked two of them. The third lock on his door had been bolted—something he had never done himself. Only a professional, using a specialized "skeleton key," could have turned that lock, Gordievsky thought. He scoured the place, looking for bugs and secret cameras, but found nothing.

After days of waiting anxiously, Gordievsky's worst fears were realized. A call came into his office from Viktor Grushko, a senior KGB official who was also Gordievsky's boss.

"Can you come over?" Grushko said. "There are two people who want to talk to you about a high-level agent penetration of Britain."

There was no refusing the order. A driver picked him up and took him not to an office but to a remote cottage outside Moscow.

Gordievsky found himself having lunch with Grushko and two men he had never seen before; obviously counterintelligence agents, he thought.

The group enjoyed a round of brandy after finishing their sandwiches, "and in a matter of seconds," Gordievsky recalled, "I was a different man.... There was no physical sensation, but instead of passing out, I was suddenly transformed into someone else.

"The next thing I knew for sure, I woke up in bed in the room across the corridor," he continued, "unable to remember anything since drinking the brandy. It was early morning—the next morning. The bed was clean, the room fresh, but I felt sick, with a severe headache."

The KGB men had drugged and interrogated him. But to their dismay, Gordievsky had passed the test. He told them nothing.

And then, mysteriously, they let him go. The KGB didn't believe him, but even under the influence of drugs, Gordievsky had somehow kept the truth from his interrogators. As a senior KGB official with colleagues and admirers throughout the Soviet government, Gordievsky could not simply be arrested; the KGB had to find solid evidence of his treachery or force him to admit it. From then on, however, their operatives would watch his every move.

"We know very well that you've been deceiving us for years," Grushko told him. "If only you knew what an unusual source we heard about you from!"

It became clear to Gordievsky that someone had turned him in, but that the KGB did not yet have the concrete evidence it needed to bring him to trial.

Gordievsky now knew what he had to do.

"There's no alternative," he convinced himself. "If I don't get out, I'm going to die. I'm as good as a dead man on holiday."

★ ★ ★

MI6's instructions laid out an "exfiltration" plan that would be difficult under the best of circumstances. But Gordievsky was a marked man, trailed by counter-intelligence teams and under constant electronic surveillance. Moscow, moreover, sat five hundred miles inside the Iron Curtain.

Also, MI6 made it clear that exfiltration was for Gordievsky alone: He would have to leave his wife and two daughters behind, to an uncertain fate. The logistics of smuggling four people safely out of the USSR were simply too daunting; in any case, neither MI6 nor Gordievsky himself could know how his family would react to learning that he was a spy for the West.

In the end, Gordievsky made the lonely and wrenching decision of the double agent: to save his own life. "With my wife and children around me," he recalled, "it was impossible to take such a harsh decision. My heart was aching so much that I could hardly bear to think about it. But slowly the conviction grew that my only real option was to flee the country."

Step one would be simple: He was to stand by a specific lamppost at seven PM on a Tuesday, holding a shopping bag. MI6 watchers checked the signal spot weekly; his presence would flip a switch, telling them to activate the escape sequence.

On his way to the signal site, Gordievsky did what trained spies called "dry cleaning," taking a meandering route over the course of three hours, stopping at stores, checking subtly for a KGB tail, and getting on and off different subway cars. By seven, Gordievsky was certain that nobody was following him.

"My instructions were to stay there long enough to be noticed," Gordievsky said, "then to withdraw to the corner and stand outside the window of a bakery." According to his instructions, his silent contact would acknowledge Gordievsky by chewing something as he passed by.

Finally, a man carrying a Harrods bag (from a department store in London) and eating a Mars candy bar appeared and stared directly into Gordievsky's eyes. MI6 had received Gordievsky's signal.

It was time for step two: the train ticket to Leningrad, the Soviet Union's second-largest city.

If Gordievsky was seen buying a train ticket, the KGB would apprehend him immediately. Once again, he made a "dry cleaning" run on the way to the station, in Moscow's Komsomolskaya Square.

Once, walking along a row of houses, he turned a corner and made a quick dash up a set of stairs to shake off anyone who might be following him. "From a window I saw a fat man hurry round the corner," he recalled, "almost running, then stop and search about him. He looked hot and uncomfortable in jacket and tie, but he was clearly no fool, for he realized that I had done something unusual."

Gordievsky had been right to exercise caution, for the mysterious man "began to speak into a small microphone fastened to his lapel. After hesitating for a moment he hurried on—and five or six seconds later a coffee-colored Lada [a Soviet-made car] nosed into view, crawling along the footpath."

He had shaken the KGB tail, and he secured his ticket.

After a final night in his apartment, Gordievsky set out on the last and most perilous leg of his exfiltration plan.

He could carry nothing that would indicate he was leaving on a long journey. On Thursday afternoon, he left his home and his possessions behind, most likely forever.

Gordievsky took off through the woods beyond his apartment complex and broke into a run. When he arrived at the station, it seemed to him that "the whole place was seething with men in uniform. I felt threatened by this totalitarian display, and for a moment my overheated imagination made me think they were looking for me."

This time, however, he had eluded his surveillance team. Gordievsky was alone, boarding a train for Leningrad—away from Moscow and toward the border, toward freedom.

After the train, Gordievsky switched to a taxi, and then—for the final leg of his solo journey—to a bus. Route E18 from Leningrad to Vyborg ran for miles through remote Russian woods. He had studied maps of this area for weeks, and he knew precisely where to get off the bus—a place marked by a large boulder right near the road. When the bus pulled away, he hid behind the boulder.

The weather was hot and muggy. "Mosquitoes tormented me," he remembered, "whining round my head in a continuous swarm: I swatted and cursed them, and one by one the minutes ticked away."

When the rendezvous time passed, Gordievsky's anxiety turned to panic. Finally, he could hear the sound of an approaching car engine: "Peering out, I saw two cars pull up right opposite. Two men got out, one of them the fellow who had passed me munching at the signal site in Moscow." His MI6 rescuers had found him!

Almost immediately, Gordievsky removed his shoes and handed them to one of the agents.

"Keep these separate, please," he said, "They may have radioactive dust on them."

In the 1980s, the KGB had begun marking suspected foreign agents with an invisible radioactive dust that could be picked up with radiation sensors. The Soviets also used the chemical compound nitrophenyl pentadienal, known as "spy dust," to tag diplomats, journalists, and anyone else they suspected of espionage; if a Soviet official tested positive for the chemical, his activities—and loyalties—would immediately attract suspicion.

Soon, Gordievsky found himself curled up in the trunk of one of the cars, racing toward the border crossing to Finland, just a few miles north of Vyborg. The MI6 agents had brought along their wives, who rode beside them in the front seats of both cars, helping provide a cover story should the Soviet guards become suspicious.

At the border post separating the Soviet Union from Finland, Gordievsky lay motionless, covered with a heavy blanket.

"All the time I was thinking, what happens if someone

opens the boot?" he recalled. (In fact, Gordievsky did not realize that his British rescuers had picked him up in a specially modified Land Rover. His hiding space had been built to look like the "hump" where the car's drive shaft normally ran; if a Soviet guard had opened the trunk, nothing would have seemed amiss.)

As the minutes ticked by, he could hear guard dogs sniffing at the car.

"Little did I know," he said, "that one of my rescuers' wives was carefully feeding the Alsatians with potato crisps to divert their attention from the car."

A short time later, the trunk popped open, and out stepped the only suspected informer ever to escape from the USSR under the noses of the KGB.

Finnish music blared from the radio, a sign that they had passed the border, out of the USSR. "I saw blue sky, white clouds, and pine trees above me," Gordievsky remembered. "Best of all, in the middle of that glorious view was the face of Joan, the architect of my escape plan, the wonderful friend who had been my case officer in England. Seeing her, I knew that my troubles were over. Thanks to the courage and ingenuity of my British friends, I had outwitted the entire might of the KGB. I was out! I was safe! I was free!"

A meeting in the Oval Office between Oleg Gordievsky and President Ronald Reagan on July 21, 1987. Reagan recorded the following entry in his diary after the meeting: "Forgot—this morning had a meeting with Col. Oleg Antonvich Gordiyevskiy (sic)—the Soviet K.G.B. officer who defected to Eng. His wife & 2 little girls were left behind. We've been trying to get them out to join him." Six years passed before Gordievsky's family could leave the Soviet Union.

Ronald Reagan Presidential Library

WANTED BY THE FBI

ESPIONAGE; INTERSTATE FLIGHT - PROBATION VIOLATION

EDWARD LEE HOWARD

FBI No. 720 744 CA2

Photograph taken 1983

Aliases: Patrick Brian, Patrick M. Brian, Patrick M. Bryan, Edward L. Houston, Roger H. Shannon

Edward Lee Howard's FBI "wanted" poster. He was never captured.

Federal Bureau of Investigation collection

THE YEAR OF THE SPY

hen Soviet leader Konstantin Chernenko passed away in March 1985, he became the third Soviet leader—following Leonid Brezhnev and Yuri Andropov—to die in three years. Chernenko, who had served in that position for a mere thirteen months, was virtually unknown in the West. Several weeks before his death, he had to be carried from his hospital bed to make one of his rare public appearances. By that point, he was too weak even to sign documents. One historian called Chernenko "an enfeebled geriatric so zombie-like as to be beyond assessing intelligence reports, alarming or not."

For the highly secretive Soviet government, a leadership merry-go-round like this was unprecedented: In the entire history of the USSR, only four men had occupied the leadership post. America's leaders found the sudden changes bewildering. "How am I supposed to get anyplace with the Russians if they keep dying on me?" President Ronald Reagan quipped.

Only weeks later, the Soviet Politburo (the main decision-making group within the Soviet Communist Party) surprised the world by electing Mikhail Gorbachev general secretary. Few people knew much about the youngest politician ever to hold that post—but his youthful appearance and energetic personality immediately attracted the attention of the international media. A committed Communist, the fifty-four-year-old Gorbachev seemed ready to make changes to the country he loved, believing that if the USSR was going to survive, it had to change its economy and open its political system to new opinions and new ideas. "It seemed," Gorbachev commented early in his term, "that our aged leaders were not especially worried about our undeniably lower living standards, our unsatisfactory way of life, and our falling behind in the field of advanced technologies."

Gorbachev called his plans for economic change *perestroika* (Russian for "restructuring"), and his goal for opening the political system *glasnost* (for "opening").

Gorbachev also claimed to want to see an end to the Cold War. Though wary of this sudden about-face, Ronald Reagan seemed willing to soften his rhetoric and take a new look at US-Soviet relations. The two leaders scheduled a summit meeting in Geneva, Switzerland, for November of that year. A thaw between America and Russia, something most leaders would have thought impossible only months earlier, seemed on the horizon.

This new, halting relationship between two old enemies would demand more of the CIA and KGB, as America and Russia asked hard questions about each other's intentions—and motives. In 1985, it was up to spies to find the answers.

But when ice starts to melt on a frozen lake, the surface can shift unpredictably. In the spring of that year, the CIA was thrown back on its heels by the first of several shattering revelations about treachery in its ranks.

On May 20, a team of FBI agents raided a Maryland hotel room where a man named John Anthony Walker was staying. Walker, America soon learned, was overseeing a massive KGB spy ring in the US Navy that stretched back eighteen years. A former naval officer, he claimed to have grown disillusioned with America's long war with Russia. "The farce of the cold war and the absurd war machine it spawned," he said, "was an ever-growing pathetic joke to me." But it was also true that Walker needed money badly, having incurred debts as the owner of a bar in Charleston, South Carolina. At some point in his naval career he realized that he had information about the American submarine fleet, and the secret codes it used to communicate, which he could trade for cash. In October 1967, he drove from his base in Norfolk, Virginia, to the Soviet embassy in Washington, DC. The skeptical KGB officer who met with him, it turned out, was a Soviet navy veteran, and he was able to determine on the spot that the documents Walker carried with him that day were genuine—and extremely valuable to the USSR. He quickly assigned one of his deputies, Oleg Kalugin, to meet with Walker regularly via dead drops and other covert methods.

In exchange for regular payments from the KGB, Walker gave the Soviets more than one million encrypted messages that revealed some of the US Navy's most sensitive information—including a top secret technology used by the Navy to track Soviet submarines. Even after he retired from the Navy, Walker continued to spy for the Soviets by recruiting his son and his brother—both naval personnel—to work with him in exchange for money. According to the *New York Times*, "it's been estimated by some intelligence experts that Mr. Walker provided enough code-data information to alter significantly the balance of power between Russia and the United States."

As Walker's betrayal sank in at the CIA, even more unwelcome news arrived from overseas—this time from the very heart of Moscow.

On June 13, Paul Stombaugh waited for his contact on a drab Moscow city block. In a few minutes, his "bren"— a CIA term for a quick meeting—would take place with Adolf Tolkachev, a Soviet military engineer who had been passing blueprints and other technical documents to the CIA since the late 1970s. Tolkachev had high-level access to the latest designs of all Soviet fighter aircraft and radar systems. Once in possession of this information, American engineers were able to anticipate the Soviets' capabilities and to design planes and missiles that could outmaneuver and outmatch them. Tolkachev's espionage helped America achieve total air superiority by the late 1980s, earning him the nickname "the Billion Dollar Spy."

Unfortunately for Stombaugh, and for Adolf Tolkachev, the legendary Major General Rem Krassilnikov had been on their trail for months. Known as the "professor of counterintelligence," Krassilnikov was one of the KGB's most skilled operatives; he had known both Kim Philby and George Blake, and he closely studied the techniques of his opponents in the West. Krassilnikov also believed passionately in the USSR. His first name, Rem, was an acronym for *revolutsky mir*, Russian for "world revolution."

The coast was clear, Stombaugh observed. He carried two shopping bags for Tolkachev, filled with ruble notes, cameras, and special drafting pens and books for Tolkachev's son, an architecture student in Moscow. The bags also contained simple items not readily available in the Soviet Union—including toothpaste.

Then "Moscow exploded around Paul Stombaugh," according to one account. The quiet urban scene was a carefully staged KGB setup. Agents tackled Stombaugh, pinning his arms behind his back in a painful "chicken wing" position often used by the KGB.

Like Marti Peterson before him, Stombaugh soon found himself in a KGB interrogation room. And an angry Krassilnikov was not ready to let the CIA agent go.

STOMBAUGH: American diplomat. I want to call the embassy. Now.

KRASSILNIKOV: You are not a diplomat, you are a spy.

STOMBAUGH: I am a diplomat.

KRASSILNIKOV: You are a spy!

Eventually, like Peterson, the KGB declared Stombaugh PNG and summarily ejected him from the Soviet Union. And like Ogorodnik, Tolkachev had actually been arrested by the KGB long before the confrontation with Stombaugh on the streets of Moscow. This time, however, Krassilnikov took special precautions. As KGB officers surrounded Tolkachev, one of them forced a thick rope between his teeth, to prevent him from biting down on a suicide pill. In fact, Tolkachev hadn't gotten that far: The poison-tipped pen still sat in his pocket.

By the middle of 1985, the KGB had thrown the CIA on the defensive. The Americans suspected that Tolkachev had been betrayed—but by whom? And who might be next? At CIA headquarters in Langley, the mood darkened.

Suddenly, out of nowhere, it seemed, a ray of light crossed its doorstep. On the morning of August 1, 1985, Colonel Vitaly Yurchenko informed the staff at the Soviet embassy compound in Rome that he would be spending the morning touring the museum exhibits in Vatican City. It was not seen as an unusual request from a senior KGB official like Yurchenko, who regularly toured the city to meet secretly with agents he was running against the CIA and other Western powers. A twenty-year veteran of the Soviet spy service, Yurchenko had traveled the world on behalf of the USSR, including a stint at the Soviet embassy in Washington, DC.

That afternoon, the phone rang on David Shorer's desk at the US embassy in Rome.

"Mr. David Shorer, I am a Soviet official who is interested—"

"Where are you now?" Shorer interrupted.

"Across the street from the entrance to your embassy," the voice said.

David Shorer wasted no time.

"Hang up the phone and walk across the street to the American embassy now. I will meet you at the main entrance."

Later that evening, the KGB issued a worldwide alert to its agents that Vitaly Yurchenko had gone missing. It came too late: Yurchenko was already onboard a CIA plane bound for Andrews Air Force Base near Washington, DC.

★ ★ ★

A cluster of the CIA's top officials waited for Yurchenko on the tarmac. Gardner "Gus" Hathaway had only recently become director of counterintelligence, having taken over the post once occupied by the notoriously paranoid James Jesus Angleton. (Just a few years earlier, Hathaway had served as chief of the Moscow station, when Marti Peterson ran the Ogorodnik case.)

Hathaway's job was to keep the CIA from being penetrated by moles from rival spy services—above all, the KGB. And one of the best ways to find out about moles was by interrogating a high-level defector like Yurchenko. If, that is, he turned out to be the real thing.

The early reports sent from Yurchenko's interview in Rome indicated that the CIA had a big fish on its hands.

Hathaway was joined by Aldrich Ames, the CIA agent in charge of counterintelligence inside the Soviet–East European Division. Ames had arrived late and seemed nervous about meeting the first major Soviet defector of his career. Together they would debrief the Soviet spy in a safe house hidden away in northern Virginia.

Yurchenko's plane arrived at Andrews. The spy descended the staircase, swarmed by CIA and FBI agents.

"Colonel Yurchenko," Ames announced, "I welcome you to the United States on behalf of the president of the United States."

At CIA headquarters in Langley, Virginia, Burton Gerber was reading a classified cable sent directly from Rome. Gerber was director of operations in the Soviet Union and Europe, the man in charge of all the Agency's spies in those areas. The cable contained the results of the initial interview conducted by David Shorer with the most important KGB defector in a generation.

CITE: ROME 22345 011405Z AUG 85
IMMEDIATE HEADQUARTERS SECRET/RESTRICTED HANDLING
WNINTEL
REF: ROME 22340

1. FURTHER TO DEBRIEFING OF KGB COLONEL
   VITALY SERGEYEVICH YURCHENKO DPOB 2 MAY
   1936 SMOLENSK, USSR. DEBRIEFING CONTINUES
   IN WALK-IN ROOM, BUT FOLLOWING SALIENT,
   POSSIBLY ACTIONABLE TAKE FROM INITIAL
   DEBRIEF OF YURCHENKO WILL BE OF SPECIAL
   INTEREST:

A. THERE [ARE] NO IMMINENT SOVIET PLANS
   TO ATTACK U.S.

B. YURCHENKO KNOWS OF U.S. VOLUNTEER
   TO KGB, CODE-NAMED "MR. ROBERT,"
   WHO [WAS] DESCRIBED AS FORMER CIA
   OFFICER PIPELINED FOR ASSIGNMENT TO
   MOSCOW BUT FIRED FOR UNSUITABILITY
   ISSUES AND POLYGRAPH PROBLEMS IN
   1983–84. YURCHENKO ADVISES THAT
   "MR. ROBERT" PROVIDED IDENTIFYING
   DATA ON SOVIET DEFENSE INDUSTRY
   SCIENTIST ADOLF TOLKACHEV
   RECENTLY ARRESTED IN MOSCOW IN JUNE
   THIS YEAR FOR ESPIONAGE ON BEHALF
   OF CIA…

   …

E. YURCHENKO ALSO REPORTS KGB HAS
   RECRUITED NSA EMPLOYEE WHO PROVIDED
   DETAILS ON SENSITIVE NSA MARITIME
   OPERATIONS AGAINST SOVIET NORTH
   SEA SUBMARINE FLEET. YURCHENKO
   CANNOT RECALL NAME OF NSA
   EMPLOYEE, BUT MET WITH VOLUNTEER
   PERSONALLY WHILE HE SERVED AT SOVIET
   EMBASSY WDC.

To prove that he had valuable information, Yurchenko had quickly offered the CIA evidence of two active Soviet moles within the US government. The information in the cable hit the CIA like a bombshell.

Gerber recognized the first mole instantly.

"It's Howard. 'Mr. Robert' is Edward Lee Howard," Gerber said. "Edward Lee Howard has betrayed us."

The mole "Mr. Robert" had been a CIA trainee several years earlier, along with his wife, Mary, who was also a CIA agent. Their first overseas assignment was a big one: The husband-and-wife team departed for Moscow to become Paul Stombaugh's replacement. They had already been briefed on the Tolkachev case when the CIA learned some unsavory things about Edward Lee Howard's past, including theft and lying on a polygraph test. Without warning, the CIA fired Howard, ending his career just as it was getting started.

"Howard left the CIA with nothing to show for his time except bitterness, a knowledge of Russian, and a head full of some of the Agency's most closely guarded secrets," wrote one chronicler of the case. An embittered Howard took those secrets, including the identity of Tolkachev, "the Billion Dollar Spy," directly to the KGB.

It took the FBI several weeks to hunt down Yurchenko's second mole, but he was soon cornered.

Ronald Pelton had left his job at the NSA in 1979. Since

then, he had been selling the NSA's secrets to the Soviets for a total of $37,000, money he used to pay off old debts. There was no evidence that Pelton felt any attraction to communism or had a personal desire to help the Soviet Union; he seemed to be motivated entirely by money.

One of the programs betrayed by Pelton was code-named IVY BELLS. Much like VENONA four decades earlier, IVY BELLS had been designed to intercept Soviet communications by siphoning them from a cable—except this time, the cable was several hundred feet below the ocean surface, in a remote and forbidding sea.

Navy divers, or "frogmen," used a mini-submarine to place a "pod" on an important Soviet underwater communications cable in the Sea of Okhotsk, north of Japan and near the eastern coast of the Soviet Union. The pod wrapped around the cable without breaking it and detected the signals through a process called induction. The pod could be released from the cable without leaving any trace of the tap.

By monitoring Soviet communications on the cable, the NSA was able to gain crucial intelligence about Soviet missile tests on the nearby Kamchatka Peninsula.

In 1981, a US spy satellite detected a group of Soviet ships on the surface, right at the spot where the IVY BELLS pod attached to the cable. Soon afterward, a US submarine determined that the pod had gone missing. Four years later, following Pelton's arrest and confession to the FBI, the CIA understood why. In 1986, Ronald Pelton was convicted of espionage and sentenced to life in prison.

Capturing Edward Lee Howard was going to be much more difficult. He was highly trained, intelligent, and one of their own: the first CIA agent to defect to the KGB.

Inside the CIA, one man in particular fretted about Howard's espionage skills. His name was Jack Platt, the very person who had taught Howard everything he knew about countersurveillance. Jack Platt's internal operations course at the Farm (the CIA's training facility in Virginia) was legendary. At the completion of the course, CIA trainees were tested by top FBI surveillance teams. In short, Edward Lee Howard understood exactly what he was up against, and he had been trained—by the CIA no less—to beat the FBI at its own game.

In September, a team of FBI "Super Gs," or specially trained surveillance agents, landed in Santa Fe, New Mexico, near Howard's home. They watched him around the clock. Yurchenko's testimony did not give the FBI enough evidence to arrest Howard—they needed hard proof of his illegal activities if they were to have any hope of building a case and bringing him to trial.

Right away, Howard knew they were trailing him. "I saw guys in baseball caps circling the house," Howard recalled. "They had no business there.

"My CIA training overrode my wishful thinking,"

Howard said, "and I also recalled one of James Bond's maxims: 'Once is coincidence. Twice is enemy action.'" By mid-September, he believed there was only one option left.

On September 21, 1985, Edward Lee Howard and his wife, Mary, crafted a plan taken straight from the internal operations course: Howard was going to "move through the gap," eluding his surveillance team in the same way that trained agents would shake their KGB watchers in Moscow.

"I fabricated the jib dummy at home on the morning of my escape," Howard recalled. "It was a crude but effective dummy, made from a sawed-off broomstick with a coat hanger for the shoulders, my wife's Styrofoam wig holder for a head, and a disguise wig I had left over from my CIA training."

"Jib" was short for "jack-in-the-box," the name given to pop-up dummies developed by the CIA to make it seem as if a passenger were riding in a car.

Howard put the jib in his car and then disconnected the brake lights, so that anyone following him would not know when the car was slowing down.

Finally, he laid one last trap for the FBI.

"I made a tape recording of my voice," Howard said, so that Mary could place a call to his doctor after the escape and play the taped message so that it would be left on the doctor's answering machine.

"It was designed to give the FBI phone-tap operators

reassurance that I was still at home and keep them off my trail."

In the late afternoon, Howard and his wife left the house. They had dinner at a local restaurant called Alfonso's, while a babysitter watched their son, Lee. Howard—knowing that his phone was tapped—even called home from the restaurant to check on his son.

All was going to plan. *I'm back in control,* Howard thought.

It was an emotional dinner for the Howards, as both knew that it would be a long time before they saw each other again. Edward Lee Howard later regretted not saying more to Mary.

"I was concentrating on the escape plan," he recalled. "I was operational."

When night began to fall, the Howards put their plan into action.

"Back at Camp Peary [the Farm]," Howard recalled, "I had practiced the jib jump over and over again under the watchful eyes of the instructors, who yelled and screamed at us until we got it right."

Mary turned sharply at an intersection, a place where a hedge ran along the right side of the road, blocking the view of anyone who might be following them. She slowed the car.

"I looked at her, she looked at me," Howard said. "A kind of frozen half second. Nothing was said."

"I moved to the outboard side of the seat, flipped up the dummy, put my hat on it, opened the door, jumped out, and shoved the door closed as I jumped."

He rolled across the sidewalk and into the hedge as Mary continued driving. When she returned home that evening, a surveillance team noted two people riding in the 1979 Oldsmobile. After she pulled into the garage, the FBI assumed that Edward Lee and Mary Howard had come home for the night.

It took the FBI more than twenty-four hours after Howard had jumped from his moving car to figure out that he had escaped. Edward Lee Howard, in CIA terms, had gone "black." Howard spent nine months on the run. In June, he walked into the Soviet embassy in Budapest, Hungary.

"We know who you are," they said. "We wondered how long it would take."

On August 7, 1986, nearly a year after his daring escape, the official Soviet news agency TASS announced that the USSR had granted Edward Lee Howard political asylum. A little over six months later, he was reunited with his wife and son, who joined him in Moscow.

★ ★ ★

In the weeks following Howard's disappearance, in August and September of 1985, Yurchenko huddled with the CIA at the safe house, telling Hathaway and Ames everything he knew about the KGB. In exchange, the Agency offered him a new life, even taking him to Montreal to meet with his Russian girlfriend, who had traveled there with the CIA's help. But when he appeared at his girlfriend's hotel room door, she rejected him, saying that she had fallen in love with a KGB colonel—not a traitor.

Heartbroken, Yurchenko returned to Washington. For the first time since his defection, he was plagued with doubts about the path his life had taken. A few weeks later, on Saturday, November 2, Yurchenko suddenly changed his mind.

"What would you do if I got up and walked out? Would you shoot me?"

Vitaly Yurchenko fired these questions at Tom Hannah, the CIA agent assigned to guard him during a shopping trip to Washington, DC. The two men were having dinner at a French restaurant in Georgetown, a neighborhood just down the hill from the sprawling Soviet embassy complex.

"No, we don't treat defectors that way," Hannah replied.

"I'll be back in fifteen or twenty minutes," Yurchenko said. "If I'm not, it's not your fault." It was a curious statement, but Tom Hannah brushed it off and let Yurchenko walk out; though he was under the care of the CIA, the KGB defector was not a prisoner.

Yurchenko then stepped out of the restaurant and

hailed a taxi heading up Wisconsin Avenue. Several minutes later, he stepped out of the car and approached the gates of the Soviet embassy. The highest-ranking KGB official ever to defect to the CIA had simply walked away.

The *rezident* of the Soviet embassy in Washington approached Victor Cherkashin, a veteran KGB officer and spy handler, as soon as Cherkashin stepped out of his car in the compound's secure parking lot.

"Yurchenko's back," he said.

It was stunning news, after three months of hand-wringing and damage control at the highest levels of the KGB.

"He's upstairs now," the *rezident* continued. "He showed up about twenty minutes ago. Said he decided to come back himself."

An astonished Cherkashin headed straight up to the room where Yurchenko was waiting.

"Congratulations," Cherkashin said. "Welcome back. You don't know how happy I am you managed to escape. How did you do it?"

"The bastards," said Yurchenko. "They kidnapped me in Rome. They drugged me. I got away as soon as I could. I'm so happy to be back. I just hope I can find support for my actions here."

Cherkashin told Yurchenko that he definitely would. He noted to himself that Yurchenko seemed completely genuine. But he didn't believe a word of Yurchenko's story.

From the moment Vitaly Yurchenko landed at Andrews Air Force Base in August, the KGB had tracked nearly every word he said, examined every Soviet secret he revealed to the Americans, and learned about every mole he uncovered in the CIA. They knew that his defection was real, and they worked around the clock to contain the fallout.

There was no question in Cherkashin's mind that Yurchenko was a traitor; the only thing he wondered was why he had come back.

For now, though—and perhaps forever—Cherkashin would go along with Yurchenko's version of events. And that's because the double agent Cherkashin was running inside the highest ranks of the CIA was far more valuable to him than punishing a single renegade KGB colonel. Protecting the true identity of the mole was Cherkashin's first task.

"Had he known that a KGB agent was telling us everything he'd been doing since his defection," Cherkashin said, "it's unlikely he'd have dared return.

"Our priority was making sure he didn't defect again before we got him to Moscow as quickly as possible," Cherkashin added. "That meant pretending to be overjoyed to see the prodigal son back on our side while posting security guards to make sure he didn't sneak out."

Before Yurchenko's departure for the USSR, the Soviets

held an international press conference at their Washington embassy, where reporters were invited to ask Yurchenko himself about the re-defection.

"I was forcibly abducted in Rome by some unknown persons," Yurchenko said. "Unconscious, I was brought from Italy to the USA. Here I was kept in isolation, forced to take drugs, and denied the possibility to get in touch with official Soviet representatives. When I was drugged...I don't know what I was saying."

Yurchenko landed in Moscow to a hero's welcome. The KGB deliberately played up his re-defection, hoping to sow confusion inside the CIA and FBI over whether he had been telling them the truth—or whether the whole episode was a carefully orchestrated KGB deception. For years after, debates raged inside the US government about Yurchenko's authenticity and over how the CIA could possibly have let him escape.

Worse, Yurchenko, Howard, and Pelton were just the beginning. In the remaining weeks of the year, more CIA informants were "rolled up" by the KGB behind the Iron Curtain; in all, ten major US agents fell to the Soviets that year, the worst losses for the CIA of the Cold War. As the year came to a close, some people inside the CIA began to fear that the problem lay not with the relative strength of the KGB but deep inside the Agency itself. Were there more traitors in their midst? they wondered. Could any of their intelligence about the "main enemy" be trusted, at this critical time? Not since the days of George Blake's double cross had the CIA found itself in such a hall of mirrors.

The news media came up with a nickname for the year 1985: "Year of the Spy."

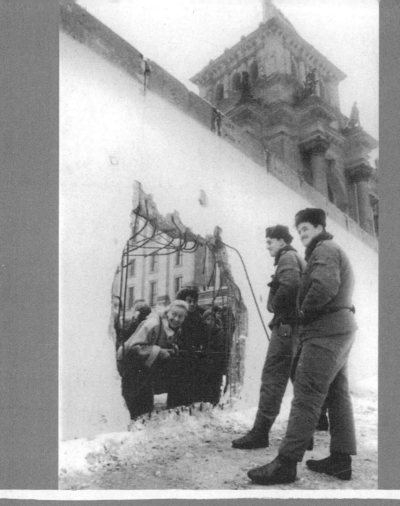

West Germans looking through a hole punched out of the Berlin Wall, January 5, 1990.

German Federal Archive

PART **4**

THAW

The first public photograph taken of Markus Wolf, during a trip he made to Stockholm in 1978.

Säpo, Sweden's national security service

THE MAN WITHOUT A FACE

O n May 28, 1990, two American gentlemen arrived at the gate of my country house," the East German spymaster recalled. "They introduced themselves with disarming candor as representatives of the CIA and presented a large box of chocolates to my wife."

Given all that had happened over the past year, Markus Wolf was hardly surprised that two CIA officials had appeared on the doorstep of what he referred to as his dacha (using the Russian term for a getaway cottage) in the village of Prenden, twenty miles from Berlin. Like many senior officials in the "workers' state" of East Germany, or the German Democratic Republic, Wolf enjoyed perks that his countrymen could only dream of—multiple homes, international travel, concert tickets, and access to Western consumer goods. Wolf and his wife, Andrea, lived a comfortable life under communism. But he always insisted that the love of his work came first and was his main motivation. "My work at the top of the intelligence service satisfied me," he said. "I was convinced of its necessity, and I was deeply committed to it."

And now communism, the only way of life he had ever known, seemed on the verge of total collapse.

History had come full circle, and the main action of the Cold War returned to where it had begun: to Germany, and to Berlin.

Wolf was there at the beginning. In 1953, when he was thirty, the newly formed Ministry for State Security, the dreaded Stasi, named Wolf as head of intelligence. In 1957, Wolf became the chief of the Hauptverwaltung Aufklärung (the Main Reconnaissance Administration), the Stasi division in charge of foreign espionage, and he held this post for nearly forty years.

East Germany's master spy built the largest espionage network in the entire world, recruiting thousands of spies, informers, and watchers. Persistence was Wolf's strength; patience, the source of his power. "Intelligence is essentially a banal trade of sifting through huge amounts of random information in a search for a single enlightening gem or illuminating link," he wrote.

Wolf specialized in infiltrating the West German government, sometimes with "Romeo spies," who would strike up romances with unsuspecting single women— many of them secretaries to powerful generals and political figures.

In one case, Wolf recruited a young man, code-named FELIX, who crossed over into West Germany and found work as a salesman for a beauty-supply company. His target was the West German chancellor himself, Konrad Adenauer. FELIX would mingle with other workers at a crowded bus stop outside the chancellor's office building. In time, through careful listening, he picked out a dark-haired woman (code-named NORMA) who worked on Adenauer's staff. "They began a friendship that soon blossomed into a romance," Wolf recalled, which enabled FELIX to funnel information to the Stasi about the inner workings of Adenauer's administration.

Wolf's most notorious recruit may have been Günter Guillaume, a Stasi spy who was sent to live in West Germany as a young man in 1956. Guillaume joined the Social Democratic Party of Germany and eventually became a trusted aide to Willy Brandt—who was first the mayor of West Berlin and then rose to become chancellor of West Germany. When the BND, the West German spy service, discovered Guillaume was a spy, the popular Brandt's political career was ruined.

Many people in West Germany hated Wolf, but he was so secretive and elusive that few outside of the Stasi had ever laid eyes on him. For that reason, Wolf earned the sinister nickname "the Man Without a Face."

Throughout the Cold War, the communist world saw its spies and spymasters come and go; Markus Wolf outlasted all of them. And now, in 1990, the system he helped create had self-destructed.

Almost thirty years earlier, East Germany's communist leaders had put up the Berlin Wall to dam the river of emigrants trying to leave the country. In 1989, the dam burst.

First, neighboring Hungary opened its border with noncommunist Austria—creating the first open border along the Iron Curtain since the start of the Cold War. East Germans snuck out this "back door" by the thousands, before the Stasi had time to prevent their departure.

Protests against the communist government broke out all over East Germany in the fall of 1989. On October 9, 70,000 people marched in Leipzig. A week later, the crowd swelled to 120,000; the following week, the protesters numbered more than 300,000. That same month, Erich Honecker, the iron-fisted East German leader, was removed by the communist leadership. His weak successor, Egon Krenz, didn't last even six weeks in power.

The end came, it seemed, almost by accident. On November 9, an East German government spokesman named Günter Schabowski gave a press conference at which he stated that travel restrictions between East and West Germany would be eased.

Toward the end of the press conference, a simple question triggered what would become one of the most legendary exchanges in the history of the Cold War:

QUESTION: (many voices) When does that go into effect?... Without a passport? Without a passport? (no, no) When is that in effect?...(confusion, voices) At what point does the regulation take effect?...

SCHABOWSKI: What?

QUESTION: When does it come into effect?

SCHABOWSKI: (Looks through his papers) **That comes into effect, according to my information, immediately, without delay** (looking through his papers further).

No one saw it coming. Had the East German government suddenly put an end to the most notorious symbol of the Cold War in Europe?

East German citizens didn't wait around to find out. By the dozens, then hundreds, then thousands, they began to assemble at the border crossings between East and West Berlin on the evening of November 9. Just days earlier, approaching the border without the correct documents would have led to arrest and imprisonment; that evening, the confused and overwhelmed border guards simply gave up and watched as thousands upon thousands of their fellow citizens streamed into West Berlin.

That night, CIA agent David Rolph—the agent who had run Adolf Tolkachev in Moscow—sent a classified cable to CIA headquarters describing the fall of the Berlin Wall. Because the Agency had no high-level agents in East Germany, Rolph's cable was America's only official source of information about the impending collapse of the East German communist state.

Sergeant Michael Rafferty was guarding Checkpoint Charlie, the precise spot where US and Soviet tanks had faced off three decades earlier when the Wall first went up.

"You'd see the people from the East pause and take a deep breath," he recalled, "before they crossed the white line because they understood what it meant. Almost everybody did and immediately they were cheered."

Night after night, East Berliners surged into West Berlin, crowding its shops, restaurants, and cafés. "What I will never forget is this," one of them commented, "the taste of my first strawberry yogurt! It tasted so good that I lived on it for a week!"

When people began chipping away at the Berlin Wall,

more joined in—including the very East German border guards who were supposed to protect it.

After years in which life seemed to stand still behind the Iron Curtain, communist East Germany unraveled with breathtaking speed. On January 15, 1990, when news spread in East Berlin that the Stasi had begun to shred its files, a large crowd of protesters rushed into the Stasi headquarters. The forbidding complex of twenty buildings employed 7,000 people; by some estimates, the Stasi archives contained more than one billion documents describing the vast network of spies and informers cultivated over four decades.

Two months later, East Germany held free elections. The Christian Democratic Union, a non-Communist party pushing for reunification with West Germany, emerged victorious. Soon afterward, Markus Wolf retreated to his country home, far away from the angry crowds in East Berlin.

★ ★ ★

The CIA man who introduced himself as Mr. Hathaway—"thin faced and graying," according to Wolf—announced that he was a personal representative of CIA director William Webster. He was the same Gus Hathaway who had been in charge of the Moscow station when Marti Peterson was arrested, and who had interrogated Vitaly Yurchenko in 1985. The CIA's counterintelligence chief retired in the late 1980s, but when the Wall fell, he rejoined the Agency to take care of some unfinished business. Accompanying him was a man named Charles—Hathaway's bodyguard, Wolf assumed.

The CIA wanted to negotiate a deal. They would offer Wolf protection, a new life away from the uncertainties and risks of post-communist Germany. And they would provide him with money—over a million US dollars.

"California is very agreeable," Hathaway offered. "Great weather all year round.

"You could have a disguise or face-lift if you would feel safer that way," Hathaway continued.

"I am happy with my looks as they are," Wolf retorted.

Wolf interjected that he could always move to Russia, where he had spent the formative years of his life.

"Don't go to Moscow," Hathaway insisted. "Life there is hard. Think of Andrea. Come to a country where things would be pleasant for you, where you can work and write quietly. In my opinion, that is only possible for you in America now."

As a seasoned recruiter of spies, Wolf knew that the Americans wanted something big from him. But what could it be? After all, the Stasi was defunct, its infamous archives looted—many of them sold off, he suspected, to the CIA itself.

Wolf mulled his options, but he knew there was something he would not trade.

"My limit is that I will not betray anyone who worked for me," he insisted. "No names."

Markus Wolf understood that, with the Cold War quickly thawing and the spy wars coming to an end, some people might want justice. He himself might be hunted. But as it turned out, the Americans had no interest in settling scores with the Stasi or even the KGB.

They were after one of their own.

"Herr Wolf," Hathaway said, "we have come because we know that you have operational information that might be useful to us in a particularly serious case. We are looking for a mole inside our operation. He has done a lot of damage. Bad things happened to us around 1985."

Now Wolf understood. The Agency had launched the most difficult kind of counterespionage campaign: the mole hunt. And they hoped that the Man Without a Face might offer them a precious clue to the identity of the traitor.

"We spoke guardedly," Wolf remembered, "about great Soviet traitors—Penkovsky, Gordievsky, Popov—men whose change of loyalties helped the Americans keep pace with Soviet espionage."

Wolf felt sympathy for Hathaway. "He was captive to the deathly puzzle he had spent his last working years trying to solve: Who was his own agency's serial traitor?

"It must have cost him dearly in pride to travel to Berlin and ask for help from a former enemy," Wolf reflected.

Hathaway continued to press Wolf on the identity of the mole. "It was clear," he said, "that the CIA was in a state of panic about its penetration."

Markus Wolf's memory was legendary. He carried code names, passwords, and secret identities in his head, afraid that storing them anywhere else might compromise his agents. But now he could not help Hathaway and the CIA, for the simple reason that he had no clue who the mole might be.

If the mole was working with the KGB, his identity was locked deep inside Lubyanka.

The CIA men offered Wolf an escape plan if he decided to change his mind and work with the Americans. Wolf's wife, Andrea, would go to the Bahnhof Zoo train station and call a specific number from a public telephone. "She was to introduce herself as Gertrud," Wolf recalled, "and say, 'I want to talk to Gustav.'" Wolf assumed that the call would connect to the CIA's Berlin station as well as to CIA headquarters in Langley.

In the end, Markus Wolf concluded that America could never be his home. "Having arrived in 1945 on one of the first flights of returning German communists from Moscow after Hitler's demise," he concluded that "it would be an ironic ending to fly out of Berlin forty-five years later under the cover of the Americans."

Still, Wolf's alternatives had narrowed. "By now," he

recalled, "the pressure was intense, and I knew that the German authorities were eager to see me behind bars. Where could I escape to, and what would be the cost of refuge? There were no compelling options, and I was running out of time."

★ ★ ★

In late September 1990, barely a week before the reunification of Germany, Markus Wolf and his wife, Andrea, left their home and fled across the border into Austria. They carried a few belongings and a secret phone number supplied by the KGB. The Russians had offered to help him as a last resort.

"It was the best of a bad bunch of offers," Wolf recalled.

"The border guards cast cursory glances at our documents and waved us on," Wolf recalled. "When we were well out of their sight, we stopped and hugged each other like children playing hooky from a strict boarding school."

For two months they were on the run, staying in small hotels or with sympathetic friends. After the reunification treaty was signed on October 3, Wolf's face started to appear on the covers of European newspapers. Where had Germany's "most wanted spy" escaped to? Somehow, nobody recognized him.

"It was an exhilarating time," he recalled, "but I knew that we could not go on forever like some German Bonnie and Clyde."

Markus Wolf finally made the call he had been avoiding.

★ ★ ★

The revolt against communism that destroyed East Germany finally spread to the Soviet Union itself. Astonishingly, one of the main instigators was Mikhail Gorbachev.

In October 1988, in a speech to the Politburo, Gorbachev took aim at his fellow communist leaders:

> The entire structure of our society and state must work
> on a legitimate basis, i.e., within the limits of the law.
> No one has the right to go beyond the boundaries of the
> law, to break the law. And the most important violator...
> is sitting here, at this table—the Politburo, and also the
> Secretariat, of the Central Committee.

In his farewell address to the Americans, in January 1989, Ronald Reagan stated that "my view is that President Gorbachev is different from previous Soviet leaders. I think he knows some of the things wrong with his society and is trying to fix them."

Two months later, the USSR held its first free elections, for the newly created Congress of People's Deputies. Non-Communist candidates won a fifth of the seats.

On June 16, 1990, at the October Theater in Moscow, an unexpected guest asked to speak to the large crowd of supporters of Democratic Platform, a new group of activists fighting for the opening of the USSR's tightly controlled political system. Some of the activists figured that Oleg Kalugin was a KGB plant sent to disrupt the event. Many more questioned his motives; after all, Kalugin was a retired KGB general and had once directed the spy service's counterintelligence operations inside Russia.

Like the Stasi in East Germany, much of the KGB's work in Russia had nothing to do with chasing foreign spies. Rather, the KGB acted as the all-powerful police force for the Soviet Communist Party—imprisoning dissenters, intimidating critics, and silencing opponents. The new wave of reformers saw the KGB as not just a symptom of the USSR's problem but the root of the problem itself.

"After the third orator," Kalugin recalled, "someone from Democratic Platform took the microphone to announce that a former KGB general was now going to address the group about reforming the secret police agency. The audience went wild."

No KGB official had ever taken a public stand against the organization inside the USSR. For Kalugin, there was no going back.

"I am from the KGB," Kalugin began. "I worked in that organization for more than thirty years and I want to tell you how the KGB works against the best interests of democratic forces in this country."

Kalugin's appearance had an electrifying effect on the

crowd and on the larger democracy movement inside Russia. He was soon speaking at rallies, giving interviews, and meeting with reformers all over the country. Once, at a huge rally right outside the Kremlin, Kalugin was struck by how rapidly the world had turned upside down: Here he was, "a KGB general...standing before a sea of humanity in Manezh Square calling for the dismantling of the KGB."

Kalugin's new public role was just beginning. Within months, he had been elected to the Congress of People's Deputies as a leading figure of the movement for democracy in Russia.

★ ★ ★

On August 18, 1991, the KGB made its last stand against Kalugin and his allies. His phone rang at six AM. A staff member from the Congress was on the line: "*Perevorot*," she said, using the Russian word for "coup."

In the middle of the night, a group of KGB and military leaders had arrested Gorbachev at his vacation dacha and announced a state of emergency. Thousands of KGB officers descended on Moscow, backed by troops and tanks. The plotters banned all newspapers, seized television and radio stations—and, ominously, ordered 300,000 pairs of handcuffs, which were shipped to Moscow.

"I stepped onto the balcony of my bedroom," Kalugin recalled. "Gazing down on the quiet courtyard and parking lot seven floors below, I saw a Zhiguli sitting off to one side of the lot in a place where few people ever park. Surveillance team, I thought."

If Kalugin was wondering what the KGB had in mind for him, he soon found out.

In the subway, on his way to his office at the Congress, a voice barked at him from behind.

"Don't turn around," a man said. "You will be arrested, but not today. I will warn you when it is coming."

The man then handed Kalugin a piece of paper. "Call me," he said. "My home phone number is written here."

As Kalugin would learn throughout the day, his mysterious protector was not the only KGB agent or soldier opposed to the coup. They joined thousands of ordinary citizens who rallied in Moscow and around the country to support Gorbachev, and democracy. When tank battalions approached the Congress, democracy protesters threw up barricades. One tank commander announced that he would protect the protesters instead of arresting the reformers.

By the next day, the plotters lost their nerve and the coup fizzled. Gorbachev was freed.

That night, as celebrations spilled out into the streets, Oleg Kalugin dialed the phone number on the piece of paper in his pocket.

"I want to thank you in person," Kalugin said.

Kalugin and a man named Ivan—a KGB agent assigned by the plotters to watch and, eventually, arrest him—toasted each other with shots of vodka in Kalugin's apartment.

"Many in the KGB hated you," Ivan said, "but there were many others like me who thought you were right."

The KGB's symbolic end arrived on August 22, 1991, not long after the failed coup. In Moscow, a crowd of over 20,000 people assembled in front of the KGB headquarters, below the statue of Felix E. Dzerzhinsky, a Communist leader of the Russian Revolution and the founder of the first secret police organization, known as the Cheka. (Dzerzhinsky was the one who said that the proper role of his police force was "the terrorization, arrests, and extermination of enemies of the revolution on the basis of their class affiliation or of their pre-revolutionary roles.")

Oleg Kalugin witnessed the scene. "A young man clambered atop the black metal statue," he recalled, "and attached a rope to Dzerzhinsky, but no amount of pulling would bring down this formidable figure." Finally, with the help of several cranes provided by the city government, the statue known locally as "Iron Felix" soon lay in pieces on the ground, as the crowd chanted "Down with the KGB!"

★ ★ ★

"And do you know what happens tomorrow?"

Rem Krassilnikov reflected on the tidal wave of change that had swept over the world he once knew. As a sign of this transformation, his conversation partner was none other than Milton Bearden of the CIA. The two senior officials had been meeting to explore ways that the CIA and KGB might work together, now that the Soviet Union was crumbling from within.

Krassilnikov continued, "Because even though we fought our way into Berlin forty-five years ago at great human cost, and even though we have been one of the four powers occupying Berlin since 1945, after tomorrow, I will need to apply for a visa to come to Berlin. Do you find irony in this?"

On December 25, 1991, Mikhail Gorbachev resigned as the last leader of the Soviet Union. As one of his final acts, Gorbachev passed the Soviet nuclear codes—which could initiate a nuclear missile launch—to Boris Yeltsin, the president of the Russian Federation. The next day, the Soviet Union itself was dissolved.

"With little fanfare," said Milton Bearden, the CIA officer who watched the final ceremony, "the detachment of Red Army soldiers had marched out on the Kremlin wall and had for the last time lowered the Hammer and Sickle, raising in its place the Russian tricolor."

It's over, Bearden thought.

"The whole thing we called the Cold War was over. And it felt pretty good. We hadn't beaten them in straight sets, not by any stretch of the imagination. But beat them we had. Our KGB adversaries had been gifted. We might not have been more gifted, but our system was, and in the end we were probably just good enough."

★ ★ ★

"You see the way things are here, Mischa," the KGB chief said. "You've been a good friend to us, but there is nothing more we can do for you here now. Who would have thought it would end like this!"

Markus Wolf had waited out the fall of communism and now watched the dissolution of his longtime protector, the KGB. His last remaining option was to go home.

German guards apprehended him when he crossed the German border from Austria. The newly reunified Federal Republic of Germany charged Markus Wolf with treason. His trial began on May 3, 1993. Many former secret agents, including Günter Guillaume, testified against him, helping expose Wolf's massive, decades-long effort to spy on the West—which reportedly involved more than 4,000 spies in West Germany alone.

Wolf's trial also sparked a debate about crimes committed during the Cold War, who should be considered guilty, and the uncertain connections between past and present.

Was Markus Wolf guilty of treason to the German people? Or was he the dutiful and respected spy chief of a country that no longer existed? "It's weird," said Heribert

Hellenbroich, a former head of the BND, the West German spy service. "The paradox is that I did the same thing. So did Klaus Kinkel when he ran the BND. And so did former President Bush when he was head of the CIA.

"Should we all stand trial, too?" he wondered.

The court convicted Markus Wolf and sentenced him to six years in prison, but he appealed its decision and won his freedom.

"I feel no guilt," Wolf commented, "because I'm accused of treason and I didn't betray my country."

★ ★ ★

In the United States, another kind of argument was raging, within the American government itself. Why had the CIA, whose "main adversary" had been the USSR and its spy service, not predicted the sudden collapse of the Soviet Union? Admiral Stansfield Turner, who headed the CIA in the late 1970s, said that the Agency "missed by a mile."

The powerful Democratic senator Daniel Patrick Moynihan called for the CIA to be disbanded. Both the House and Senate Intelligence Committees "introduced bills calling for sweeping reorganization of the entire intelligence apparatus of the government."

The Cold War was over, and America, in the eyes of its leaders and in the view of millions of people around the world, had won. But this "victory" shook the CIA—the agency that led the fight in that nearly fifty-year war—to its core. Battered, its reputation deeply dented, the CIA looked inward. The end of the spy wars left the CIA with a lot of cleaning up to do and unresolved questions to be reckoned with.

★

MOLE HUNT

In November 1989, CIA officer Diana Worthen visited her old friend Aldrich Ames at his home on North Randolph Street in Arlington, Virginia. What she saw shocked her. Three years earlier, Ames was scraping by in a modest one-bedroom rental apartment. Now his lavish home included landscaped gardens, an expensive Jaguar sports car in the driveway, and a maid.

Worthen's field-agent training set her mind buzzing about what she had seen. How could a career CIA agent like Ames, a man who had never made more than $60,000 per year, live such a life of luxury?

When she returned later to CIA headquarters, Worthen visited the Office of Security in the Agency's Counterintelligence Center. The young agent on duty there quietly opened an internal investigation into Aldrich Ames. He discovered two things: Ames, a midlevel agent, had paid $540,000 in cash for his home on North Randolph Street. And he had occasionally made large cash deposits into his checking account—far more money than he earned from his salary at the CIA.

The Agency's spy hunters now had a lead on a possible mole and an explanation for all the losses the CIA had suffered since 1985.

And then—nothing happened. The ghost of James Jesus Angleton still cast a shadow over the CIA; few people accepted that the Agency had been infiltrated, and even fewer wanted to go back to the days of Angleton's feverish mole hunts, which had crippled the CIA's operations for nearly a decade. The investigation crawled forward without attracting much attention.

Aldrich Ames not only continued to work at the CIA, but—incredibly—in 1990 the CIA even assigned him to work at the Counterintelligence Center itself, where all the secrets about CIA operations against the KGB were stored.

The CIA simply did not want to believe that one of its own could have betrayed its deepest secrets.

★ ★ ★

In 1985, Aldrich Ames's career had stalled, and for good reason. His personnel file painted the picture of a CIA agent who was deeply knowledgeable about the KGB but also careless, clumsy, and erratic.

Years earlier, on his way to meet a Soviet agent in New York City, Ames accidentally left his briefcase on the subway. The case contained a secret compartment, in which

Ames had stashed a document describing the CIA's relationship with the spy, along with his photograph; Ames never found it again. Once, his boss reprimanded him for leaving a safe packed with top secret documents open overnight. Ames often drank alcohol at lunch, came back to the office in a fog, and would sleep at his desk. At a US embassy party in Bogotá, Colombia, he drank so much that he stumbled through the gardens and woke up the next morning on the sidewalk next to his apartment. Inside the Agency, his fellow officers considered him lazy and unreliable.

Yet Ames stayed under the radar, avoiding serious trouble with his employer. In fact, his shoddy work may well have been the key to his success as a double agent. No one believed Aldrich Ames could do something so well.

Unlike many of the double agents who preceded him, Aldrich Ames did not turn to spying because he was attracted to communism. Ames looked around his Washington, DC, suburb and felt envious of his wealthy neighbors enjoying the booming US economy of the 1980s. Simply put, he wanted more money. And in early 1985, Ames realized that he did possess something of great value: the CIA's deepest secrets.

To test his theory, Ames prepared a document with the names of two Soviet intelligence officers who had approached the CIA to work as double agents for the United States.

"Fifty thousand dollars was an appropriate sum," according to Ames. "It was a sum they [the KGB] had frequently offered Agency officers in recruitment approaches over the past five, ten years.

"I was sure they would respond positively," he added, "and they did."

Ames gambled that as chief of counterintelligence for the Soviet division of the CIA, approaching the KGB couldn't be simpler. He told his colleagues that he was cultivating a new Soviet source. And then he walked into the Soviet embassy on Wisconsin Avenue in Washington, DC, and handed the guard a letter for the KGB agent in charge.

In exchange for his information, the KGB gave Ames a package containing five hundred $100 bills.

★ ★ ★

The first taste of real money gave Aldrich Ames a hunger for more. And, as his colleague Diana Worthen later learned, Ames wasn't shy about spending lavishly; on the contrary, he openly—and carelessly—flaunted his newfound affluence, sporting expensive new suits at CIA headquarters and showing off pricey dental work.

From his office in the Soviet–East European Division, Ames pulled secret files on every Soviet agent who had switched sides and was now working with the CIA. When he was done, he had compiled a six-pound stack of documents. Ames stored these in plastic bags, which he put inside his briefcase. On June 13, 1985, he simply walked out of CIA headquarters with his precious and dangerous cargo and drove home.

On June 13, Ames arranged to meet with the KGB at Chadwicks, a restaurant in Washington, DC.

The deputy head of the KGB *rezidentura* at the Soviet embassy, Victor Cherkashin, believed that this meeting was "the moment we hit the mother lode, the moment the tables turned on the CIA.

"Fate," he reflected, "had rewarded me for the days and nights of hard work I'd put in over the previous three decades."

It was the perfect setup. Ames had permission from the Central Intelligence Agency to meet with the very man to whom he was handing over the Agency's most important Soviet agents.

Ames sat at a window table with Cherkashin and with Sergei Chuvakhin, a legitimate Soviet diplomat who would act as his "cutout," or go-between with the KGB.

"He hesitated," Cherkashin recalled, "then took out a notepad and paper and began writing down a list of names. He tore out the page and handed it to me. I was shocked. That piece of paper contained more information about CIA espionage than had ever before been presented in a single communication." Ames had given the KGB the names of thirteen Soviet informers working for the CIA— including Colonel Oleg Gordievsky.

"It was a catalogue of virtually every CIA asset within the Soviet Union," Cherkashin said.

The KGB wasted almost no time. Two of the spies unmasked by Ames—Oleg Gordievsky and Sergei Bokhan—escaped with their lives. The Soviets executed all the others.

Aldrich Ames met with his cutout again and again during the summer and fall of 1985—exactly the same period when Ames was the main CIA interrogator of Vitaly Yurchenko. Everything Yurchenko said to the CIA made its way back to the KGB.

KGB general Oleg Kalugin later wrote that the Soviet Politburo believed that Ames "has presented information of such value that he should be paid as much as possible."

From 1985 until 1994, the KGB paid Aldrich Ames more than $2 million. For nine years, Ames delivered to the Soviets a steady stream of secrets, betraying more than one hundred CIA operations against the KGB. In forty years of battling against the CIA, the Soviets had never garnered so much intelligence from a single secret agent.

"Ames was the top spy ever," Kalugin said.

★ ★ ★

One agent inside the CIA never gave up on the idea that a mole had burrowed into the heart of the America spy service. In 1993, Paul Redmond held the same counter-intelligence post once occupied by Aldrich Ames. He realized that after so many years of hunches and suspicions, the time had come to bring in the experts, the spy hunters of the Federal Bureau of Investigation.

Working together, the CIA and FBI conducted a painstaking search, cross-referencing everyone who had access to the names of the agents executed by the KGB. Slowly, the list grew smaller.

The figure of Aldrich Ames rose to the top.

Redmond ordered a review of Ames's bank records, which quickly revealed that Ames had deposited over $1.5 million in cash over the previous eight years.

The FBI then made a fateful discovery. The Bureau had kept surveillance videotapes of comings and goings into the Soviet embassy, filmed from a secret location across the street. They managed to piece together every time Ames had walked into the building to meet with his KGB contact. They then matched those dates to his bank records. Their analysis revealed that, following each visit to the Soviet embassy, Ames had made a large cash deposit into one of his accounts. The only logical conclusion was that he had traded something for that much money. If Redmond had any doubts that Ames had gone over to the KGB, they now evaporated.

The investigation moved into a new and final phase.

On July 20, 1993, the FBI summoned Ames to a meeting at FBI headquarters, supposedly related to his counterintelligence work. While Ames sat in the meeting, a team of FBI technical experts placed a homing device inside his

Jaguar. From then on, a special FBI surveillance team—the same "Super Gs" who followed Edward Lee Howard in Santa Fe—tracked all of Ames's movements, hoping to catch him in the act of clearing a dead drop or meeting with his KGB contact.

Meanwhile, FBI agents tapped Aldrich Ames's phones and picked through his office at the CIA. They bugged his home and listened in on his conversations with his wife. But it wasn't until they searched behind the house on North Randolph Street, late one night, that the last pieces of evidence fell into their hands. In his final, careless act as a double agent, Ames had left incriminating notes to and from the KGB in his trash can.

★ ★ ★

"Okay. Go ahead."

With that command from FBI headquarters, the operation to arrest Aldrich Ames swung into action. On February 21, 1994, more than a hundred agents and other personnel quietly staked out the neighborhood around his house. A smaller team of eight agents moved in to catch the KGB mole.

First, a call from Ames's CIA office lured Ames out of his house.

"Something important has just turned up," Ames's boss said. "It has a direct bearing on the Moscow trip.

"You better come into the office. I think you need to see it now."

Ames jumped into his Jaguar and started down North Randolph Street. At the next intersection, his way was blocked by two unmarked cars, which had stopped side by side.

Two other cars pulled in behind him. FBI agents and SWAT officers swarmed Ames's car.

"Get out of the car," one of them barked. "You're under arrest for espionage."

As officers placed handcuffs on his wrists, Ames cried out, "What's this all about? You're making a big mistake! You must have the wrong man!"

★ ★ ★

On April 28, Aldrich Ames pleaded guilty in federal court to espionage. In a packed courtroom in Alexandria, Virginia, the judge sentenced Ames to life in prison, without the possibility of parole. Soon afterward, Prisoner 40087-083 settled into the federal penitentiary in Terre Haute, Indiana, where he remains today.

Five years later, Ames gave a prison interview that offered a glimpse into his motivations. "The reasons that I did what I did in April of 1985," Ames said, "were personal, banal, and amounted really to a kind of greed and folly. As simple as that.... I mean, you might as well ask

Aldrich Ames is led from the federal courthouse in Alexandria, Virginia, following his sentencing in 1994.

Getty Images

why a middle-aged man with no criminal record might go and put a paper bag over his head and rob a bank."

The final case of the Cold War was now shut, and the mysteries surrounding the Year of the Spy had been solved.

A short time after the trial and conviction, one of Ames's disillusioned CIA colleagues reflected on the larger meaning of his capture and sentencing.

"The last chapter had been written," she said, "the book could be closed."

★

ACKNOWLEDGMENTS

Though spies often toil alone, their work depends on a large and sometimes invisible network of dependable allies and friendly faces. *Spies* was no different. I rely on daily inspiration and support from Patty, Owen, and Emmett Favreau. Tanya McKinnon of McKinnon Literary has been my instigator and guide. Lisa Yoskowitz, editorial director at Little, Brown Books for Young Readers, shaped *Spies* in more ways than I can count, challenging both my thinking and my writing. Lisa's editorial colleague Hannah Milton improved the manuscript immensely through her perceptive reading and comments. My sincere thanks go out as well to others at Little, Brown who contributed to this book in myriad ways, including Karina Granda, Jen Graham, and David Koral.

I am grateful to David Fielder, Dinny Montrowl, and Gary Montrowl for a chain of communication that connected me with Marti Peterson, and to Marti herself for helpful comments and permission to use her images. Jane Chisholm, who appears in these pages as a young girl seated with her mother Janet in a Moscow park, not only provided that photograph but also sharpened the accuracy of the story surrounding it with much-needed details.

The idea for this book was sparked by a perceptive comment from a young friend, during a family outing in Little Falls Park, on the Maryland–Washington, DC, line—not far from the spot where Aldrich Ames and his KGB handlers exchanged documents via dead drop. I hope this young reader is pleased with the outcome. I'm also indebted to her dad, Andrew Weiss, for technical and moral support as I traced a path from idea to book.

KGB: KEY FACTS

DATE FOUNDED: 1954

FIRST DIRECTOR: Ivan Aleksandrovich Serov

PREDECESSOR ORGANIZATIONS:
Cheka (secret police organization)
     1917–1922
NKVD (People's Commissariat for Internal Affairs)
     1917–1930; 1934–1946
NKGB (People's Commissariat for State Security)
     1941–1943
MGB (Ministry for State Security)
     1943–1953

HEADQUARTERS: Lubyanka Building, Moscow

INTERNAL ORGANIZATION:
Much of what is known about the Cold War–era KGB came
from information provided by defectors from the Soviet
Union. It has been estimated that the total number of KGB
personnel ranged from 500,000 to as many as 700,000 people,
but there is no independent source to verify those figures.
     The main operations of the KGB were organized within
"chief directorates":

First Chief Directorate
Foreign espionage and intelligence gathering.

Second Chief Directorate
Counterintelligence and political control of all people (citizens and foreigners) inside the USSR.

Third Chief Directorate
Military counterintelligence and surveillance of dissent within the Soviet armed forces.

Fourth Chief Directorate
Security for transportation and transportation infrastructure.

Fifth Chief Directorate
Founded in the 1960s to supplement the role of the Second Chief Directorate: to watch over Soviet citizens and to suppress dissent by writers, lawyers, artists, religious groups, and other individuals and organizations.

Sixth Chief Directorate
Economic and industrial counterintelligence—protecting Soviet industry from foreign spies.

Seventh Chief Directorate
Surveillance of Soviet citizens and foreigners inside the USSR.

Eighth Chief Directorate
Communications globally, including cryptological equipment. Additional, smaller directorates provided border security and security for senior officials and their families; conducted technological research for espionage equipment (including poisons); and carried out other functions.

CIA: KEY FACTS

DATE FOUNDED: 1947

FIRST DIRECTOR: Allen Dulles

PREDECESSOR ORGANIZATIONS:
Office of the Coordinator of Information
    1941–1942
Office of Strategic Services (OSS)
    1942–1945
Central Intelligence Group
    1946–1947

HEADQUARTERS: Langley, Virginia

INTERNAL ORGANIZATION:
In general, the CIA has been organized around two activities: analysis and operations. CIA analysts specialize in up-to-date knowledge of foreign countries, threats to the United States, weapons systems, and other areas. CIA operations officers work in the clandestine or operations division and generally operate overseas, conducting espionage, intelligence gathering, or paramilitary activities on the part of the United States.

1950s: Led by the director of Central Intelligence (DCI), the CIA at the height of the Cold War had three main divisions.

Even this basic description of the CIA's internal organization was classified until 2000:

OPERATIONS (OVERSEAS ESPIONAGE OFFICES)
Office of Special Operations
Office of Policy Coordination
Office of Operations

CENTRAL INTELLIGENCE (ANALYTICAL OFFICES)
Office of Collection and Dissemination
Office of Research and Development
Office of National Estimates
Office of Intelligence Coordination
Office of Special Services
Office of Scientific Intelligence

ADMINISTRATION
Security Office
Administration Services Office
Communication Office
Today: The CIA now has five main directorates, as well as a larger number of specialized mission centers that focus on key challenges (e.g., terrorism) and regions (Europe, North Africa, etc.):

Directorates
Analysis Directorate
Digital Innovation Directorate
Operations Directorate (formerly the National Clandestine Service)
Science and Technology Directorate
Support Directorate

Mission Centers
Africa
Counterintelligence
Counterterrorism
Weapons and Counterproliferation
Regional Centers

RUSSIAN ESPIONAGE SINCE THE END OF THE COLD WAR

After the attempted coup on Mikhail Gorbachev, the KGB's reputation began a downward slide that would eventually lead to its dissolution in 1991. The KGB had been a massive organization, responsible for policing opponents of the Soviet regime, guarding the USSR's borders, spying on foreign countries, and monitoring foreign spies inside the USSR. It was also the main source of support for the Communist Party. In order for a new democratic government to take root, many Russians believed, the old system had to be completely dismantled.

Under President Boris Yeltsin, the new Russian Federation replaced the KGB with the Federal Counterintelligence Service (a national police force, akin to the FBI) and the Foreign Intelligence Service (responsible for overseas intelligence gathering). Other former functions of the KGB, such as border security and presidential protection, were parceled out to still more new agencies, creating an "alphabet soup" of police and security organizations. On the surface, at least, it seemed that the all-powerful spy agency had been demolished and that Russia was on its way to a more open future, with many of the individual freedoms taken for granted in the West.

However, within just a few years, these changes began to seem like a mirage. The new security agencies of the Russian state—staffed in most cases by former employees of the KGB—did not let go of their old powers. Russians still chafed under the intrusive and seemingly omnipresent police forces. And Yeltsin, far from bringing them under control, relied on former spies more and more as his own presidency struggled to get its footing in the early 1990s. In 1995, he established the Federal Security Service, or FSB, combining many of the remnants of the old KGB.

Russia experienced profound instability in these early years, as its economy transitioned from communism to a free-market system, and its people became accustomed to new ways of living and working—not all of them welcome. In this turbulent time, one particular group of people had the personal connections, and inside knowledge of government, to get ahead: the former officers of the KGB.

One ex–KGB official was especially adept at navigating the stormy seas of Russian life in the 1990s. Vladimir Putin had served as a foreign intelligence officer for the KGB in the 1970s and '80s; according to his autobiography, he was present in Berlin for the democracy demonstrations that brought down the Berlin Wall, and he took charge of burning KGB files so that the demonstrators could not get their hands on them. After the fall of the Soviet Union, Putin became involved in local politics in Leningrad and then joined the inner circle of Boris Yeltsin's administration. In 1999, Yeltsin appointed Putin as head of the Federal Security Service, which had continued to grow since 1995. And in December of that year, Yeltsin unexpectedly announced his resignation—and tapped Putin as acting president of the Russian Federation. Less than one year later, Russians overwhelmingly elected Putin president for a four-year term.

Under Putin's leadership, Russia's security services continued to grow in power and influence. And in the new century, they finally began to flex their muscles again overseas, with major operations in the heart of the most powerful countries in the world.

In October 2006, two Russian men met with Alexander Litvinenko at the Millennium Hotel in London, not far from the US embassy. Litvinenko had been an officer in the FSB and left Moscow for England in 2000, where he became an outspoken critic of Vladimir Putin and a consultant to MI6 (helping the British spy agency grapple with the problem of Russian mafia or organized crime activities around the world). During the brief meeting, Litvinenko drank a cup of green tea and then the men parted ways. A little more than two weeks later, Litvinenko lay dying of a mysterious illness in a London hospital. In the investigation that followed, MI6 discovered that he had been poisoned by a highly radioactive substance called polonium—and they traced it back to a laboratory run by the FSB. Litvinenko died on November 23.

In a similar incident, on March 4, 2018, British police found a former KGB agent—and MI6 informer—named Sergei Skripal slumped on a bench in the city of Salisbury, next to his daughter. Both were unconscious but alive, poisoned by a highly toxic nerve agent developed by the Russian military. They survived, but Russia, it seemed, was sending a message that disloyalty from its former agents would not be tolerated.

In 2016, Russia's spy services launched their biggest gambit since the end of the Cold War. Their target was their old adversary, the United States. (See "The CIA Since the End of the Cold War" for further details.)

THE CIA SINCE THE END
OF THE COLD WAR

The Central Intelligence Agency had been established to fight the "main enemy," and when the Soviet Union dissolved in 1991, many agents felt a sudden loss of purpose. Milton Bearden, a longtime CIA officer who was in charge of the Agency's Soviet–East European Division at the time of the USSR's collapse, commented that the Agency "was not an institution. It was a mission. And the mission was a crusade. Then you took the Soviet Union away from us and there wasn't anything else."

For much of the 1990s, the CIA drifted. Veteran spies left or retired. In the six-year period from 1991 to 1997, the Agency had five different directors, as one after another failed to define a new mission for American espionage. And where the United States faced new foreign policy challenges—in countries as different as Somalia, Bosnia, and Iraq—the Agency often found that it lacked even the most basic ability to gather intelligence. In Somalia, where the United States had sent a large military force in late

1992 to help stabilize the country and prevent a famine, one senior CIA official remarked that "we had no facts.

"There was no intelligence network," he added.

Above all, the CIA's leaders worried about the decline of HUMINT, or the human intelligence gathered by real spies, "on the ground." They had good reason to be concerned. For it was during the 1990s that a new and ominous threat to the United States first made its appearance, in the person of a Saudi radical named Osama bin Laden and his network of lieutenants called al Qaeda.

In the early 1990s, the CIA's counterterrorism division employed barely one hundred people. When al Qaeda set off a bomb in the basement of the World Trade Center in New York City in 1993, the Agency had few leads overseas that its agents could pursue. By September 11, 2001, only five CIA analysts were assigned to track Osama bin Laden. And when al Qaeda struck again, the CIA—at the time the world's largest and most sophisticated spy agency—was caught completely off guard.

In the aftermath of the attacks on New York and Washington, DC, the CIA scrambled to retool itself for the new war on global terrorism.

For the next decade, the CIA struggled to rebuild its reputation—along with its ability to anticipate and prevent future attacks on the US homeland. But the war on terror also gave the CIA a new lease on life. Counterterrorism had become the heart of its operations, a role that garnered the support of presidents, Congress, and the American people. And in place of the traditional spy, a new kind of secret warrior emerged from the shadows: unmanned Predator drones, armed with deadly Hellfire missiles and able to reach even remote areas of Afghanistan, Iraq, Somalia, Yemen, or wherever suspected terrorists lurked. CIA operators, often working from a command center inside CIA headquarters itself, guided these weapons to their intended targets.

Once again, however, the changing currents of history caught America's spies off guard. The CIA's oldest adversary, whose power and influence inside Russia had been growing under Vladimir Putin, launched new covert attacks on its former foe.

In 2016, a major campaign orchestrated by Russian spy agencies attempted to interfere with the US presidential campaign, spreading false information via Facebook and Twitter, hacking the Democratic National Committee's computer servers, and—allegedly—secretly helping the campaign of Donald Trump. Putin's motives, like the espionage campaign itself, were shrouded in deceptions and half-truths. But many experts believe that Russia, after a quarter century of playing second fiddle to the United States on the global stage, badly wanted to embarrass America and possibly even influence its support for NATO—an organization that still keeps Russian power in check.

And it was becoming painfully clear that the CIA's ability to respond to Russia was as weak as it had been in the years following Oleg Penkovsky's arrest. In early 2018, the media reported that a broad range of CIA informants in Moscow had suddenly gone silent—most likely as the result of Vladimir Putin's aggressive campaign of counter-espionage. In July of that same year, the FBI arrested a Russian woman named Maria Butina, charging her with acting as an illegal agent for Russia in the United States as part of Russia's campaign to influence American politics. For years, Butina had worked for Putin's government in the United States to help forge relationships between Russian diplomats and American politicians, acting as a "spotter"—a spy who passes on information to other officials in Russia's espionage services.

Only weeks after Butina's sentencing in an American courtroom, Russia arrested an American man named Paul Whelan in Moscow, charging him with spying for the United States. Some people in the US government expressed concern that Whelan's arrest was a simple tit for tat, a signal that Russia would not stand by while its own agents were tracked down in the United States. Before Whelan had even been charged formally, the prospect of a prisoner exchange—a common Cold War practice that had not been used for nearly thirty years—had been voiced openly by some officials and media commentators.

To veteran CIA agents, the simmering tensions between

America and Russia felt eerily familiar. John Sipher, a former CIA station chief who had worked in Moscow, went so far as to argue that Putin had revived the old Soviet "intelligence state," a government whose power stemmed from a dense network of large and secretive spy services. But what would that mean for the CIA? The lessons of the Cold War, once consigned to the history books and to the memories of aging spies, suddenly seemed shockingly relevant—a prologue, perhaps, to a new and ominous showdown between old enemies.

COLD WAR TIMELINE

FEBRUARY 1946:
George Kennan sends the "Long Telegram."

MARCH 1946:
Winston Churchill gives the "Iron Curtain" speech in Fulton, Missouri.

MARCH 1947:
The "Truman Doctrine" announced.

JUNE 1947:
The Marshall Plan.

JUNE 24, 1948–SEPTEMBER 30, 1949:
Berlin Blockade and Berlin Airlift.

APRIL 1949:
NATO (North Atlantic Treaty Organization) founded.

SEPTEMBER 1949:
CIA founded.

SEPTEMBER 1949:
The Soviets conduct a successful atomic test.

SEPTEMBER-OCTOBER 1949:
West and East Germany are founded as separate countries.

OCTOBER 1949:
Communist forces led by Mao Zedong take over China.

APRIL 1950:
NSC-68 presented to President Truman, providing the blueprint for America's Cold War military buildup.

1950-1953:
The Korean War.

NOVEMBER 1952:
The United States detonates a hydrogen bomb.

MARCH 1953:
Joseph Stalin dies. Nikita Khrushchev emerges as his successor.

AUGUST 1953:
The Soviet Union tests the hydrogen bomb.

MARCH 1954:
KGB founded.

MAY 1955:
Warsaw Pact founded.

OCTOBER 4, 1957:
Sputnik launched.

MAY 1960:
The U-2 incident.

APRIL 1961:
Bay of Pigs debacle.

AUGUST 13, 1961:
Berlin Wall erected.

OCTOBER 18-29, 1962:
The thirteen days of the Cuban Missile Crisis.

MARCH 1965:
US troops sent to Vietnam in large numbers.

AUGUST 1968:
Soviet troops invade Czechoslovakia and depose the reform
government of Alexander Dubček.

1969-1979:
Period of détente, or a thawing of relations, between the
United States and the USSR.

DECEMBER 1979:
Soviet invasion of Afghanistan.

MARCH 1983:
Announcement of Strategic Defense Initiative, or "Star Wars."

SEPTEMBER 1983:
Korean Air Lines flight 007 shot down by a Soviet fighter.

MARCH 15, 1989:
Mikhail Gorbachev elected Soviet president.

JUNE-NOVEMBER 1989:
Fall of communism in Eastern Europe; Berlin Wall falls on
November 9.

COLD WAR GLOSSARY

arms race
The competition between the United States and the Soviet Union, beginning in 1949, to build more and stronger nuclear weapons, in an effort to achieve military superiority over each other during the Cold War.

Bay of Pigs
The name given to a failed invasion of Cuba by a force of 1,400 anticommunist Cuban expatriates on April 17, 1961. Sponsored by the CIA, the invasion was intended to spark an uprising that would overthrow the Cuban leader, Fidel Castro, but instead resulted in a major international embarrassment for the United States and for President John F. Kennedy.

Berlin Airlift
After the Soviet Union cut off the western part of Berlin in June 1948, the United States responded with a massive airlift of food and other essential supplies. From June 1948 until September 1949, the Americans flew thousands of relief missions to Tempelhof Airport in Berlin, keeping the Western sector alive during the blockade.

Berlin Wall
A permanent barrier separating East Berlin and West Berlin and surrounding all of West Berlin, constructed by the East German communist government on August 13, 1963. The wall

was passable only through a series of militarized checkpoints. It was topped with barbed wire and buffered on the Eastern (communist) side by a "death strip," which prevented people and vehicles from crossing. More than two hundred people were killed attempting to sneak over the wall during the Cold War. It was demolished by protesters during the democracy movement that seized East Germany in the fall of 1989.

Bikini Atoll
A small island chain in the South Pacific that was the site of American atomic tests in the late 1940s and early 1950s. The Castle Bravo test on March 1, 1954, yielded a nuclear explosion that was one thousand times as strong as the atomic bombs dropped on Hiroshima and Nagasaki in 1945.

capitalism
An economic system in which companies are privately owned and run for the purpose of making a profit, and that supports the free trade of goods and services.

Checkpoint Charlie
A famous checkpoint in the Berlin Wall connecting West Berlin with communist East Berlin. It is now part of a museum in Berlin's Dahlem neighborhood.

CIA
The Central Intelligence Agency, the US government organization charged with collecting and analyzing intelligence about foreign countries and other threats to American security abroad. The CIA is based on a large campus in Langley, Virginia, near Washington, DC.

communism
An economic system in which economic activity and the means of production (companies, factories, etc.) are owned and

controlled by the state, for the purpose of protecting the interests of working people and achieving a level of social equality.

containment
A concept embraced by American leaders in the early part of the Cold War that argued that the United States should not negotiate with communist countries but rather seek to "contain" them by force, to prevent the spread of communism to other places.

détente
The deliberate easing of tensions between the United States and the USSR in the late 1960s and 1970s, accompanied by arms negotiations talks and other bilateral treaties.

deterrence theory
The idea that by building up a massive store of weapons—especially nuclear weapons—a country could deter an enemy from daring to attack.

double agent
A spy who pretends to work for one country while secretly working for its opponent. Famous double agents during the Cold War included Kim Philby, George Blake, and Aldrich Ames.

Duck and Cover
A civil defense film widely distributed to American schoolchildren in the 1950s, teaching them what to do in the event of a nuclear attack. Footage of the film may be viewed at the Library of Congress website at https://www.loc.gov/item/mbrs 01836081/.

espionage
The act of spying, or secretly gathering information about an adversary.

fallout shelter

A small enclosed space designed to protect occupants from nuclear fallout, radioactive material that covers a wide area following a nuclear explosion. Fallout shelters were promoted in the United States in the 1950s and 1960s as part of the Civil Defense Program, to protect American citizens in the event of a nuclear war with the Soviet Union.

first strike

A preemptive nuclear strike that is intended to completely eliminate the possibility of any retaliation by the enemy, by using overwhelming destructive force. Many strategic planners doubted the possibility of a fully effective first strike, which led to the concept of **deterrence** through **mutual assured destruction**.

free world

An expression used in the West during the Cold War to describe noncommunist nations.

GDR

The English initials for the German Democratic Republic (in German, the DDR or Deutsche Demokratische Republik), the rigid communist state, founded in 1949, that reunified with West Germany in 1990. Sometimes referred to simply as East Germany.

glasnost

Russian for "openness," a term promoted by Soviet leader Mikhail Gorbachev in the 1980s describing his goal of creating more transparency in the Communist government, and more public discussion and criticism of Soviet policies inside the USSR.

Hollywood Ten

A group of screenwriters and directors who were suspected of being communist sympathizers in 1946 and 1947. They were subpoenaed by **HUAC** (see below) and refused to testify before Congress, citing their First Amendment right to free speech. All ten were convicted of contempt of Congress, fired from their jobs in Hollywood, and prevented from working in the film industry for many years.

HUAC

The House Un-American Activities Committee, a committee of the US House of Representatives.

human intelligence (HUMINT)

A term used to describe intelligence that is gathered by spies, using the traditional techniques of spycraft. HUMINT operations generally require gradual, in-depth knowledge of a place or country, by spies who have extensive specialized training. Many of the most productive espionage operations of the Cold War were HUMINT operations.

hydrogen bomb

The common term used to describe a thermonuclear weapon, a type of atomic bomb that uses a fusion explosion (of hydrogen atoms), creating a blast that is much larger and more powerful than the fission bombs dropped on Hiroshima and Nagasaki in August 1945.

ICBM

Intercontinental ballistic missile, a type of nuclear missile developed in the 1950s that could travel thousands of miles in less than an hour. ICBMs had an enormous impact on nuclear deterrence strategy and sharply influenced the way that ordinary people in American and the Soviet Union perceived the threat of nuclear war.

Iron Curtain

A term first coined by British prime minister Winston Churchill in a speech in Fulton, Missouri, on March 5, 1946, referring to the Soviet Union's control of most of Eastern Europe. It became part of popular speech in the United States when describing the dividing line between East and West.

KGB

The Komitet Gosudarstvennoy Bezopasnosti, Russian for Committee for State Security, the main internal-security, intelligence-gathering, and secret police force for the Soviet Union, from 1954 until 1991.

Long Telegram

An 8,000-word telegram sent to the US State Department in February 1946 by George Kennan, a senior official at the American embassy in Moscow. The telegram described the motivations and goals of the Soviet leadership; along with other writings by Kennan, it is credited with outlining the policy of "containment," which defined US policy toward the USSR in the early Cold War.

Marshall Plan

The unofficial term for the European Recovery Program (ERP), launched by the United States in 1948 to help the struggling economies of Europe. The Marshall Plan eventually provided more than $12 billion in aid to European nations, enabling many of them to recover from the devastation of World War II.

McCarthyism

Named for Wisconsin senator Joseph McCarthy, a movement that sought to identify and prosecute or marginalize supposed Communists living in the United States. The term is now used to describe unjust or unwarranted attacks on someone for his or her political beliefs.

MI5

The term used to refer to the Security Service, Britain's domestic counterintelligence and national police agency, which is charged with dealing with threats inside the country. The name derives from the official designation of the service as "Military Intelligence—Section Five."

MI6

The term used to refer to the Secret Intelligence Service (SIS), Britain's foreign or overseas spying agency. The name derives from the official designation of the service as "Military Intelligence—Section Six."

mutual assured destruction

The theory that, should one power use nuclear weapons against the other, it would lead to total annihilation on both sides.

NATO

The North Atlantic Treaty Organization, a military alliance of Western democracies founded in 1949 for the purpose of providing mutual defense against a Soviet attack.

NSC-68

A secret memo presented to President Harry Truman on April 14, 1950, by the National Security Council (the name refers to National Security Council report number 68). The memo argued for a massive military buildup by the United States to counter the Soviet threat around the world, including a rapid escalation in the development of the hydrogen bomb. The document is considered to be the main blueprint for America's decision to escalate its confrontation with the USSR.

perestroika

A Russian term meaning "restructuring," which referred to the plan promoted by Soviet leader Mikhail Gorbachev to make the country's economy more efficient and competitive with global markets.

Politburo
The "political bureau" of the Communist Party of the Soviet Union. During the Soviet era, the Politburo was the highest policy-making authority in the country.

red scare
The period of fear, rumor, and panic in the United States during the late 1940s, following accusations by Elizabeth Bentley, Whittaker Chambers, and others that Communists had infiltrated the American government and other key institutions (including especially the movie business). This is sometimes referred to as the second red scare, following an earlier, similar period after World War I in 1919–20.

signals intelligence (SIGINT)
Intelligence gathering through the interception of electronic or other signals, whether through tapping cables (as in the VENONA project or Operation Gold) or by intercepting wireless or Internet-based communications.

Soviet bloc
A group of countries formally allied with (or controlled by) the Soviet Union during the Cold War, including Poland, East Germany, Czechoslovakia, Hungary, Romania, and Bulgaria.

Sputnik
The world's first satellite, measuring approximately thirty inches in diameter, which was launched into space by the USSR on October 4, 1957. *Sputnik* set into motion what became known as the "space race" between America and the Soviet Union.

Stasi

The German nickname for the Ministry for State Security, or Ministerium für Staatssicherheit, the powerful East German spy service responsible for both internal (inside the GDR) and external espionage operations. Stasi agents and informers watched over the entire East German population; in 1989, its headquarters were sacked by a large crowd of pro-democracy protesters.

Truman Doctrine

A Cold War policy articulated by President Harry Truman in a speech to Congress on March 12, 1947, that argued that America must counter the expansion of Soviet influence anywhere in the world. The Truman Doctrine was first put to the test when the United States decided to send economic and military aid to Greece and Turkey in 1948 to help their governments fight against communist insurgencies.

Warsaw Pact

A military alliance of communist nations established in 1955 under the leadership of the USSR, which included Albania, Bulgaria, Czechoslovakia, East Germany, Hungary, Poland, and Romania. Often viewed as the USSR's response to NATO. It was disbanded in 1991.

GLOSSARY OF KEY ESPIONAGE TECHNIQUES

brush pass

The brush pass involved more specialized physical training than the dead drop. With the brush pass, two agents pass one another in a public, open space and touch only briefly, but just enough to hand off documents, film canisters, or other small packages. The key is making the pass look like a natural or accidental encounter rather than an intentional exchange.

CIA agent Haviland Smith perfected the brush pass technique by studying with a professional magician. He once demonstrated it in the lobby of the Mayflower Hotel in Washington while being observed by the deputy chief of the CIA—who could not detect what had happened. Smith shook out his raincoat hem with his left hand while handing a package to a second agent with his right, creating enough of a distraction to make the brush pass all but invisible.

car toss

The car toss involves throwing a small package through an open car window, usually after a car has turned a corner and is briefly out of sight of a surveillance team. It is a basic technique for passing secret material from a vehicle to an agent, in a hostile environment.

covert image

The Technical Services Division (TSD) of the CIA devised a way for agents inside the Soviet Union to transmit messages, blueprints, or other documents via the regular mail. Using a dead drop, agents were provided with a roll of "stripping film," a clear layer of light-sensitive film that could be used to create simple exposures when pressed against a document. Once the agent created an exposure, she or he would then bleach the image so it would be only faintly visible. The bleached, clear photograph was then fastened to a standard tourist postcard featuring images from inside the Soviet Union; with images in the background, the bleached exposure was all but invisible. The agent then mailed the postcard, with an innocuous message on the back, to an address in the United States—where the image was peeled off and printed by CIA technical staff. This method was used to send Soviet missile blueprints from deep inside the USSR.

cutout

A cutout is a person who acts as an intermediary between a spy or informer and his or her handler or source. Cutouts were used throughout the Cold War to protect valuable spies or informers. For example, an East German informer for the CIA might use a local Berlin contact as a cutout, or go-between, keeping her or him one step removed from a CIA contact—who might be known to the Stasi or KGB.

dangle

A dangle is a spy from one country who pretends to offer his or her services as a double agent to an enemy country. When a dangle is successful, the fake double agent can then feed false or misleading information to the enemy, who believes that it is receiving top secret intelligence about its opponent. When Yurchenko defected to the United States in 1985, some people in the CIA suspected that he was a dangle sent by the KGB and that his revelations were intended to sow confusion inside the American spy service.

dead drop

At its simplest application, a dead drop involves one agent leaving a message or other package (including money, documents, equipment, or other materials) at an agreed-upon location, where a second agent can then pick it up. The dead drop prevents two agents from having to come into physical contact, which may be noticed by an enemy's counterespionage service.

Usually, an agent indicates a drop will happen through some sort of advance signal, such as a chalk mark on a mailbox. And when the drop is "cleared" by the second agent, she or he also leaves a mark to indicate this has occurred.

More sophisticated dead drops involve specially manufactured containers made to look like logs, rocks, or pieces of garbage. Some agents went to great lengths to repel intruders from a dead-drop container—including smearing it with dirt or even dog feces.

dissolving paper

Dissolving paper was produced in small notepads and used to pass messages, often written in code. Made of a water-soluble compound, a dissolving paper note could simply be dropped in a drink, or in a puddle, and its message would disappear along with the paper.

jack-in-the-box

Sometimes known as a "jib" or "jib dummy," this simple device—a dummy in the shape of a human from the waist up—makes it appear as if a passenger is seated next to the driver. It is meant to fool a surveillance team into thinking that a passenger is still riding in a car, after she or he has snuck out the passenger-side door.

microdot

Microdots are tiny photographs of a document or other text that are usually no more than one millimeter in diameter, or approximately the size of a period on a printed page. Since they cannot be read (or in most cases perceived) by the naked eye, they are common devices for sending instructions or other information secretly. Microdots can be hidden in a letter, a piece of currency, or on a postage stamp. Spies carried microdot readers to enlarge the microdot text and make it readable. Microdots were created by special cameras that reduced images down to a tiny size.

one-time pad

The one-time pad was a basic communications tool used by spies during the Cold War, based on principles of cryptography, or secret code writing. There were two copies of a one-time pad: one held by the sender of a message, and the other held by the recipient. The sender would translate a message into secret code, using a randomly generated "key" that existed only on the one-time pad. The recipient would then decode the message using his or her copy of the pad; after one use, both people would destroy the pad. Because the recipient is the only person holding the same "key," the one-time pad system is generally considered the only unbreakable code system for secret communications.

one-way voice link (OWVL)

OWVL was a communication method conducted via shortwave radio, used by both Western and Eastern espionage services. "Numbers stations" across Europe would broadcast a nondescript female voice, reading sets of numbers that were sometimes broken by musical interludes or other forms of punctuation. The number sets contained encoded information for spies in the field who were instructed to tune in—using widely available shortwave radio sets—at specific days and times.

secret identities

Inside the Soviet Union, every person was required to carry identification forms and "internal passports" for moving around inside the country. Police or security forces might request these at any time. The documents also included information about a person's job and military service.

CIA agents sent inside a "denied area," such as the USSR, had to have not only accurately produced documents (as forgeries were easily spotted) but a credible "legend," or life history, according to veteran CIA agent Harry Rositzke. "Each agent's legend, or fictional life history, both supported and was supported by his documents. Once he landed and became another Soviet citizen on his way from one place to another, he had to be ready to talk about himself, his past, and his plans.... Each agent realized that once his words or acts prompted police suspicion, he was through."

subminiature camera

Subminiature cameras are extremely small cameras, sometimes in the shape of a different object (for example, a pen), which were used frequently by spies to photograph secret documents. The double agent George Blake used a Minox subminiature camera to photograph documents in his MI6 office in London. In the early 1970s, the CIA's Office of Technical Services (OTS) developed the T-100 subminiature camera specifically for TRIGON, the Soviet informer later captured in Moscow.

"taking out the laundry"

"Taking out the laundry" is a CIA expression for a countersurveillance run, which refers to the process of walking or driving a route, circling back, and taking sudden detours, all with the goal of checking whether one is being followed by a surveillance team from an enemy spy service. A successful run will convince an agent that she or he is "clean" and can proceed with an operation.

NOTES

PROLOGUE: SEEING GHOSTS

1–3 The account of Ken Seacrest's mission is drawn from Robert Wallace and H. Keith Melton, *Spycraft: The Secret History of the CIA's Spytechs, from Communism to Al-Qaeda* (New York: Dutton, 2008), chapter 11.

8 "We wouldn't say much, especially with the kids there": Wallace and Melton, *Spycraft*, page 145.

8 "You developed an intuition": Ibid., page 148.

9 "The specific manhole eventually selected for an entry point": Ibid., page 140.

1: THE DEFECTOR

14 "Hiroshima has shaken the whole world": David Holloway, *Stalin and the Bomb: The Soviet Union and Atomic Energy, 1939–1956* (New Haven, CT: Yale University Press, 1994), page 132.

14–15 "They want to force us to accept their plans": Melvyn Leffler, *For the Soul of Mankind: The United States, The Soviet Union, and the Cold War* (New York: Hill and Wang, 2008), page 78.

16 *If the Russian secret police knew what I was about to do*: Elizabeth Bentley, *Out of Bondage: The Story of Elizabeth Bentley* (New York: Devin-Adair Company, 1951), page 287.

16 "I'd like to see the agent in charge": Kathryn S. Olmsted, *Red Spy Queen: A Biography of Elizabeth Bentley* (Chapel Hill: University of North Carolina Press, 2002), page 90.

16 "only one remedy is left—the most drastic one": Ibid., page 94.

17 "Here's some Moscow gold": Ibid., page 101.

18 "A new world was coming": Ibid., page 13.

19 "Underground methods were by now beginning to seem quite natural to me": Bentley, *Out of Bondage*, page 103.

22 "According to the plan, I was to enter the theater": Ibid., page 147.

24 "There wasn't any question in my mind": Olmsted, *Red Spy Queen*, page 100.

24 "FROM NEW YORK TO DIRECTOR AND SAC URGENT": FBI cable quoted in ibid., page 100.

26 "an appeal to war with the USSR": Interview with Joseph Stalin, *Pravda*, March 1946.

29 "cease immediately their connection with all persons known to Bentley": November 23, 1945, NKVD cable quoted in Olmsted, *Red Spy Queen*, page 106.

29 "Because of the successful delivery of that message": Ibid., page 106.

30–31 "But was he in the employ of the Federal Government?": Testimony quoted in *Hearings Before the Committee on Un-American Activities, United States House of Representatives, Eightieth Congress, Second Session*, August 1, 1948.

31 "lady spy," "Comrade Woman," "nutmeg Mata Hari," and the "blonde and blue-eyed": Newspaper excerpts appear in Olmsted, *Red Spy Queen*, pages 134–35.

2: THE SPY HUNTERS

35 "Every counterintelligence man's dream": Robert J. Lamphere and Tom Shachtman, *The FBI-KGB War: A Special Agent's Story* (New York: Random House, 1986), page 79.

36 "We were near and yet so far": Ibid., page 41.

36 "square-jawed, broad-shouldered, thick black hair": Howard Blum, *In the Enemy's House: The Secret Saga of the FBI Agent and the Code Breaker Who Caught the Russian Spies* (New York: Harper, 2018), page 12.

36–37 "I liked criminal cases": Lamphere and Shachtman, *The FBI-KGB War*, page 19.

37 "I'd like to take charge of the messages the ASA sent over": Ibid., page 79.

37 "The KGB messages were to change my life": Ibid.

40 "a sort of magpie attitude to facts": Meredith Gardner, quoted in Bart Barnes, "Meredith Knox Gardner, Army Code Breaker, Dies," *Washington Post*, August 15, 2002.

41 "From the first I was curious as to how Gardner": Lamphere and Shachtman, *The FBI-KGB War*, page 84.

41 "You'll find Meredith Gardner a shy, introverted loner": Ibid., page 82.

42 "I told him I was intensely interested in what he was doing": Ibid.

43 "in the most excited mood I'd ever seen him display": Ibid., page 85.

44 "We are convinced that our remaining in Berlin is essential": General Lucius D. Clay, *The Papers of General Lucius D. Clay: Germany, 1945–1949*, vol. 2, ed. Jean Edward Smith (Bloomington: Indiana University Press, 1974), page 677.

47 "Should Russia use the relatively simple and completely proven process": Michael D. Gordin, *Red Cloud at Dawn: Truman, Stalin, and the End of the Atomic Monopoly* (New York: Farrar Straus & Giroux, 2009), page 256.

47–48 "Had they been aided in their effort": Lamphere and Shachtman, *The FBI-KGB War*, page 132.

48 "I stood in the vestibule of the enemy's house": Ibid., page 86.

49 "It became immediately obvious to me": Ibid., page 134.

50 "I became convinced that Klaus Fuchs was the prime suspect": Ibid., page 135.

51 "When dominoes are lined up": Blum, *In the Enemy's House*, page 237.

52 "I have here in my hand...a list of names": Senator Joseph McCarthy, speaking before the Ohio County Republican Women's Club in Wheeling, West Virginia, February 9, 1950.

3: THE DOUBLE

55 "One by one they tiptoed out": George Blake, *No Other Choice: An Autobiography* (New York: Simon & Schuster, 1991), page 121.

55 "I felt certain that if South Korea was allowed to fall": Harry S. Truman, *Memoirs of Harry S. Truman, Years of Trial and Hope* (New York: Doubleday, 1956), page 333.

56 Communism was the declared enemy of God: Blake, *No Other Choice*, page 45.

57–58 "The first day of the war was one of confusion and conflicting reports": Ibid., page 122.

58 "After all we had heard about the Communists": Ibid., page 126.

58 "There we were put up in derelict army huts": Ibid., page 128.

59–60 "The inhabitants throughout the village and in the fields": *New York Times* correspondent quoted in Bruce Cumings, *The Korean War: A History* (New York: Modern Library, 2010), page 30.

60 "We walked all day through wild mountain country": Ibid., page 132.

60 "I remembered how in Holland, during the war": Ibid., page 141.

61 "I could have won the war in Korea in a maximum of ten days": General Douglas MacArthur, quoted in Jim Lucas and Bob Considine, "Texts of Accounts by Lucas and Considine on Interviews with MacArthur in 1954," *New York Times*, April 9, 1964.

62 "turned me from a man of conventional political views": Blake, *No Other Choice*, page 138.

62–63 "People discussed, disputed, and imagined alternative political and economic orders": Leffler, *For the Soul of Mankind*, page 78.

63 "I put my finger to my lips as I handed him a folded note": Blake, *No Other Choice*, page 142.

64 "a big burly man of about forty or forty-five": Ibid., page 143.

64 "George stood out from the motley crew in the camp": Nikolai Loenko, quoted in Helen Womack, "British Traitor George Blake 'Hooked by KGB Sweets,'" *Independent*, April 18, 1992.

65 "Having been through a rather unusual experience": Blake, *No Other Choice*, page 156.

67 "There was much speculation": Ibid., page 160.

68 "It was too near to the bone": Ibid., page 162.

68 "In order to meet me at seven o'clock in the evening": Ibid., page 161.

68–69 "He was very charming": Roger Hermiston, *The Greatest Traitor: The Secret Lives of Agent George Blake* (London: Aurum Press, 2013), page 154.

69 "This was the sort of marriage that SIS welcomed": Blake, *No Other Choice*, page 165.

69 "it became automatic": Ibid., page 162.

70 "This was just one more clandestine meeting": Ibid., page 173.

70–71 "I quickly jumped in": Ibid., page 173.

71 "For some time my Soviet contact and I had been discussing": Ibid., page 175.

4: CAPITAL OF THE COLD WAR

75 an "American James Bond": Bayard Stockton, *Flawed Patriot: The Rise and Fall of CIA Legend Bill Harvey* (Washington, DC: Potomac Books, 2006), page 119.

75 "odd looking, with protruding eyes": Lamphere and Shachtman, *The FBI-KGB War*, page 61.

76 "a bloated alcoholic with the manners of a comically corrupt cop": Ben Macintyre, *A Spy Among Friends: Kim Philby and the Great Betrayal* (New York: Broadway Books, 2015), page 145.

76 "a Wild West approach to intelligence": Blake, *No Other Choice*, page 21.

76 "When you need 'em, you need 'em in a hurry": David Stafford, *Spies Beneath Berlin* (London: Thistle Publishing, 2013), page 49.

77 "an excellent knowledge of Russian espionage": Stockton, *Flawed Patriot*, page 19.

79 "We sense with all our faculties": Dwight D. Eisenhower, first inaugural address, January 20, 1953.

79 "Whether you like it or not, history is on our side": Nikita Khrushchev, speech to foreign envoys at the Polish embassy in Moscow, November 18, 1956. Reported in the *New York Times* and other news outlets on the same date.

82 The Nummer Mädchen story is based on an account in David
    Murphy, Sergei Kondrachev, and George Bailey, *Battleground
    Berlin: CIA vs. KGB in the Cold War* (New Haven, CT: Yale
    University Press, 1997), page 211.

83 "through the construction of a subterranean passage approximately
    1,800 feet in length": CIA report quoted in ibid., page 213.

86 "a bonanza": Stafford, *Spies Beneath Berlin*, page 139.

88 "Look at that": Murphy, Kondrachev, and Bailey, *Battleground
    Berlin*, page 231.

89 "if they missed his call": Ibid., page 343.

90 "The excitement at BOB was palpable": Ibid.

94 "For an instant in time I was free and alone": Blake, *No Other
    Choice*, page 244.

96 "They can launch the *Sputnik*, but you can't get a green vegetable
    in the middle of summer": Markus Wolf, *Man Without a Face:
    The Autobiography of Communism's Greatest Spymaster* (New York:
    PublicAffairs, 1999), page 112.

96 "The booming economy in West Germany": Letter from Walter
    Ulbricht to Nikita Khrushchev, January 18, 1961, Wilson Center
    Digital Archive.

5: THE PILOT

99 "ninety percent of our hard intelligence" Michael R. Beschloss,
    May-Day: Eisenhower, Khrushchev, and the U-2 Affair (New York:
    Harper & Row, 1986), page 5.

100 "Ascent was rapid and spectacular": Francis Gary Powers,
    Operation Overflight: A Memoir of the U-2 Incident (Washington,
    DC: Potomac Books, 2003), page 18.

101 "It was a cruel assumption": Beschloss, *May-Day*, page 8.

101 "Do you want the silver dollar?": Ibid., page 14.

104 "Dad, I left my heart up there": Powers, *Operation Overflight*,
    page 4.

104 "I hadn't really proved myself": Ibid., page 9.

104 "I was amazed": Ibid., page xv.

105 "I was able to get a look at every blade of grass in the Soviet Union": Beschloss, *May-Day*, page 5.

108 "Who would have thought that the capitalists would invite me": Sergei Khrushchev, *Khrushchev on Khrushchev: An Inside Account of the Man and His Era* (New York: Little, Brown and Company, 1990), page 356.

108 "the clouds of war have begun to disperse": Beschloss, *May-Day*, page 223.

108 "If one of these planes is shot down": Ibid., page 34.

109 "I wondered how the Russians felt": Powers, *Operation Overflight*, page 59.

110 "My God, I've had it now": Ibid., page 61.

110 "Suddenly I was free": Ibid., page 63.

111 "I was completely unprepared": Ibid., page 70.

111 "It seemed useless to deny it": Ibid.

112 "Comrade Deputies": Beschloss, *May-Day*, page 43.

113 "Comrades, I must let you in on a secret": Ibid., page 60.

114 "the Americans have made fools of themselves": *News Chronicle*, London, cited in Beschloss, *May-Day*, page 250.

114 "I had thought the president sincerely wanted to change his policies": Ibid., page ix.

114 "It seemed designed to be as uncomfortable as possible": Powers, *Operation Overflight*, page 81.

114 "No one knew where I was": Ibid., page 85.

115 "What is your unit called": Ibid., page 88.

116 "Neither of my parents had ever been outside the United States": Ibid., page 131.

117 "this crew-cut, diffident, simple, rather polite man": Ian MacDougall, BBC Radio report on Powers trial, August 1960.

118 "the difference in behavior of Airman Powers and Nathan Hale": Beschloss, *May-Day*, page 335.

118 "Only as I was being led from the courtroom": Powers, *Operation Overflight*, page 158.

118 "Supper the first night": Ibid., page 170.

119 "Jim D. is back": Beschloss, *May-Day*, page 348.

120 "His was the first familiar face": Powers, *Operation Overflight*, page 237.

120 "You're Francis Gary Powers": Ibid.

120 "Powers and Abel moved forward": James B. Donovan, *Strangers on a Bridge: The Case of Colonel Abel and Francis Gary Powers* (New York: Scribner, 2015), page 422.

6: MISSILES

122 "I have tried to get in touch with other Americans", Jerrold L. Schecter and Peter S. Deriabin, *The Spy Who Saved the World: How a Soviet Colonel Changed the Course of the Cold War* (New York: Scribner, 1992), page 6.

122 "I cannot go to the American embassy myself": Ibid., page 6.

123 "gets a lot of stuff like this from tourists": Ibid., page 9.

124 "My dear Sir!": Translation of first letter from Oleg Penkovsky to the US government, quoted in Jeremy Duns, *Dead Drop: The True Story of Oleg Penkovsky and the Cold War's Most Dangerous Operation* (New York: Simon & Schuster, 2013), page 21.

126 "After all, how could anyone present the identities": Clarence Ashley, *CIA SpyMaster: Kisevalter, the Agency's Top Case Officer, Who Handled Penkovsky and Popov* (Gretna, LA: Pelican Publishing, 2004), page 145.

127 "turning out missiles like sausages!": John L. Gaddis, *The Cold War: A New History* (New York: Penguin Books, 2006), page 69.

127 "If I need some material fast or an idea fast": Odd Arne Westad, *The Cold War: A World History* (New York: Basic Books, 2017), page 301.

128 "My God, we don't have an operation here": Ashley, *CIA SpyMaster*, page 151.

129 "I can't believe it, Greville": Greville Wynne, *The Man from Moscow* (London: Hutchinson of London, 1967), page 145.

130 "henceforth I consider myself to be a soldier": Oleg Penkovsky, written CIA contract, cited in Schechter and Deriabin, *The Spy Who Saved the World*, page 94.

131 "a fit of intelligence lunacy": Duns, *Dead Drop*, page 94.

135 "Kennedy is a boy in small pants": Nikita Khrushchev, quoted in "Once Secret Berlin Wall Papers Released," *Washington Post*, October 27, 2011.

136–37 "far from being defensive and of short range": Wallace and Melton, *Spycraft*, page 34.

137 "On Tuesday morning, October 16, 1962, shortly after 9:00": Robert F. Kennedy, *Thirteen Days: A Memoir of the Cuban Missile Crisis* (New York: W. W. Norton, 1969), page 13.

137 "scariest presidential address in all of US history": Martin J. Sherwin, "One Step from Nuclear War: The Cuban Missile Crisis at 50, In Search of Historical Perspective." *Prologue* 44, no. 2 (Fall 2012).

138 "we will not prematurely or unnecessarily risk the costs of worldwide nuclear war": John F. Kennedy, presidential address, October 22, 1962, 7:00 EST.

139 "It was just the most devastating event in world history...*that somehow didn't happen*": Sherwin, "One Step From Nuclear War."

140 "For that brief and critical moment in time": Wallace and Melton, *Spycraft*, page 34.

142 "This proposition may come as something of a surprise to you": Schechter and Deriabin, *The Spy Who Saved the World*, page 371.

142 "does not communicate with an enemy intelligence service": Ibid.

7: MOSCOW RULES

149 "Ogorodnik 'felt more in control over his life than he ever had'": Martha D. Peterson, *The Widow Spy: My CIA Journey From the Jungles of Laos to Prison in Moscow* (Wilmington, NC: Red Canary Press, 2012), page 119.

151 "The craftsmanship and the technology that went into making the lens assembly was something that may never be repeated": Wallace and Melton, *Spycraft*, page 90.

152 "no one had shoes resoled in Moscow": Peterson, *The Widow Spy*, page 99.

152 "I soon discovered I had a significant advantage in casing operational sites by not having surveillance": Ibid., page 156.

154 "He suggested I not let the male case officers' bluster fool me": Ibid., page 163.

155 "I was prepared to make this drop": Ibid., page 101.

157 "I felt sorry as well as fear for him": Ibid., page 174.

158–59 "All was quiet": Ibid., page 213.

159 "My question was whether I was going to be raped, or mugged, or worse": Ibid., page 213.

159 "They smelled bad": Ibid., page 214.

159 "You can't hold me": Ibid., page 214.

161 "I wonder how many KGB officers lost their jobs": Ibid., page 225.

162 "I knew that some thought I had become sloppy": Ibid., page 231.

162 "I greatly admire your courage": Ibid., page 234.

8: WAR GAMES

167 "I intended to let the Soviets know that we were going to spend what it took to stay ahead of them in the arms race": Ronald E. Powaski, *The Cold War: The United States and the Soviet Union 1917–1991* (New York: Oxford University Press, 1998), page 233.

168 "Inside the Embassy, life was dominated by a terrible paranoia about bugging": Oleg Gordievsky, *Next Stop Execution: The Autobiography of Oleg Gordievsky* (New York: Macmillan, 1995), page 296.

169 "Once clear of the Embassy": Ibid., page 302.

169–70 "Because Leila had grown up very much a Soviet girl": Ibid., page 15.

170 "I saw the queues, the shortages, the filthiness of public lavatories, the bureaucracy": Ibid., page 209.

172 "when there are obvious indications of preparations to begin military operations": Secret KGB report quoted in Christopher Andrew and Oleg Gordievsky, *Comrade Kryuchkov's Instructions: Top Secret Files on KGB Foreign Operations, 1975–1985* (Palo Alto: Stanford University Press, 1993), page 79.

173–74 "Do you suppose they really believe that?": Benjamin Fischer, "A Cold War Conundrum: The 1983 Cold War Scare," CIA Center for the Study of Intelligence.

174 "the thunderbolt struck": Gordievsky, *Next Stop Execution*, page 367.

175 "Then he made a telephone call": Ibid., page 370.

176 "Can you come over?": Ibid., page 377.

176 "and in a matter of seconds": Ibid., page 379.

177 "We know very well that you've been deceiving us for years": Ibid., page 383.

177 "There's no alternative": Ibid., page 394.

178 "With my wife and children around me": Ibid., page 391.

178 "My instructions were to stay there long enough to be noticed": Ibid., page 18.

179 "From a window I saw a fat man hurry around the corner": Ibid., page 18.

180 "the whole place was seething with men in uniform": Ibid., page 22.

181 "Peering out, I saw two cars pull up right opposite": Ibid., page 30.

181 "Keep these separate, please": Ibid., page 31.

181–82 "All the time I was thinking": Ibid., page 33.

182 "I saw blue sky, white clouds, and pine trees above me": Ibid., page 33.

9: THE YEAR OF THE SPY

185 "an enfeebled geriatric so zombie-like": Gaddis, *The Cold War*, page 228.

185 "How am I supposed to get anyplace with the Russians": Thomas Blanton and Svetlana Savranskaya, *The Last Superpower Summits: Gorbachev, Reagan, and Bush* (New York: CEU Press, 2016), page 9.

185 "It seemed that our aged leaders were not especially worried": Gaddis, *The Cold War*, page 233.

186–87 "The farce of the cold war": John Walker quoted in John Prados, "The John Walker Spy Ring and the U.S. Navy's Biggest Betrayal," *Naval History*, June 2010.

187 "it's been estimated by some intelligence experts": John J. O'Connor, "American Spies in Pursuit of the American Dream," *New York Times*, February 4, 1990.

189 "Moscow exploded around Paul Stombaugh": Milt Bearden and James Risen, *The Main Enemy: The Inside Story of the CIA's Final Showdown with the KGB* (New York: Presidio Press, 2004), page 17.

189 "American diplomat. I want to call the embassy. Now.": David E. Hoffman, *The Billion Dollar Spy: A True Story of Cold War Espionage and Betrayal* (New York: Basic Books, 2005), page 235.

190 "Mr. David Shorer, I am a Soviet official": Bearden and Risen, *The Main Enemy*, page 73.

192 "Colonel Yurchenko, I welcome you to the United States": Ibid., page 73.

192–93 IMMEDIATE HEADQUARTERS SECRET/RESTRICTED HANDLING: Ibid., page 76.

194 "It's Howard. 'Mr. Robert' is Edward Lee Howard": Ibid., page 76.

194 "Howard left the CIA with nothing to show for his time except bitterness": Ibid., page 84.

196 "I saw guys in baseball caps circling the house": David Wise, *The Spy Who Got Away: The Inside Story of Edward Lee Howard, the CIA Agent Who Betrayed His Country's Secrets and Escaped to Moscow* (New York: Random House, 1988), page 184.

197 "I fabricated the jib dummy at home": Edward Howard, *Safe House: The Compelling Memoirs of the Only CIA Spy to Seek Asylum in Russia* (Washington, DC: National Press Publications, 1995), page 86.

197 "I made a tape recording of my voice": Ibid., page 87.

198 "I was concentrating on the escape plan": Ibid., page 88.

198 "Back at Camp Peary I had practiced the jib jump": Ibid., page 88.

199 "We know who you are": Wise, *The Spy Who Got Away*, page 228.

200 "What would you do if I got up and walked out?": Viktor Cherkashin and Gregory Feifer, *Spy Handler: Memoir of a KGB*

Officer—The True Story of the Man Who Recruited Robert Hanssen and Aldrich Ames (New York: Basic Books, 2005), page 166.

202 "Had he known that a KGB agent was telling us everything he'd been doing": Ibid., page 169.

203 "I was forcibly abducted in Rome by some unknown persons": Bearden and Risen, *The Main Enemy*, page 141.

10: THE MAN WITHOUT A FACE

207 "On May 28, 1990, two American gentlemen arrived at the gate": Wolf, *Man Without a Face*, page 9.

208 "My work at the top of the intelligence service satisfied me": Ibid., page 112.

208–09 "Intelligence is essentially a banal trade": Ibid., page 110.

209 "They began a friendship that soon blossomed into a romance": Ibid., page 138.

211 "When does that go into effect?…": Günter Schabowski, Press Conference in the GDR International Press Center, November 9, 1989, Wilson Center Digital Archive, International History Declassified.

212 "You'd see the people from the East pause and take a deep breath": Christopher Hilton, *The Wall: The People's Story* (Mount Pleasant, SC: The History Press, 2011), page 361.

213 "Thin faced and graying": Wolf, *Man Without a Face*, page 9.

214 "California is very agreeable": Ibid., page 11.

215 "My limit is that I will not betray anyone who worked for me": Ibid., page 13.

215 "we have come because we know that you have operational information": Ibid., page 14.

216 "It must have cost him dearly in pride to travel to Berlin": Ibid., page 17.

216 "She was to introduce herself as Gertrud": Ibid., page 15.

216–17 "By now, the pressure was intense": Ibid., page 21.

217 "It was the best of a bad bunch of offers": Ibid., page 364.

217 "It was an exhilarating time": Ibid., page 365.

218 "The entire structure of our society and state must work on a legitimate basis": Mikhail Gorbachev speech, quoted in Westad, *The Cold War*, page 551.

219 "After the third orator": Oleg Kalugin, *Spymaster: My Thirty-Two Years in Intelligence and Espionage Against the West* (New York: Basic Books, 2009), page 387.

220 "a KGB general...standing before a sea of humanity": Ibid., page 389.

220 "*Perevorot*": Ibid., page 406.

221 "Don't turn around": Ibid., page 412.

221 "I want to thank you in person": Ibid., page 415.

222 "And do you know what happens tomorrow?": Bearden and Risen, *The Main Enemy*, page 455.

223 "With little fanfare": Ibid., page 522.

223 "The whole thing we called the Cold War was over": Ibid., page 522.

224 "You see the way things are here, Mischa": Wolf, *Man Without a Face*, page 367.

225 "The paradox is that I did the same thing": Heribert Hellenbroich, quoted in the *Los Angeles Times*, "On Trial: Spymaster Without a Country," May 4, 1993.

225 "I feel no guilt": Ibid.

225 "introduced bills calling for sweeping reorganization of the entire intelligence apparatus of the Government": Elaine Sciolino, "Director Admits C.I.A. Fell Short in Predicting the Soviet Collapse," *New York Times*, May 21, 1992.

EPILOGUE: MOLE HUNT

230 "Fifty thousand dollars was an appropriate sum": Tim Weiner, David Johnston, and Neil A. Lewis, *Betrayal: The Story of Aldrich Ames, an American Spy* (New York: Random House, 1995), page 36.

231 "the moment we hit the mother lode": Cherkashin and Feifer, *Spy Handler*, page 24.

232 "It was a catalogue of virtually every CIA asset within the Soviet Union": Ibid., page 29.

232 "has presented information of such value that he should be paid as much as possible": Weiner, Johnston, and Lewis, *Betrayal*, page 68.

234 "Okay. Go ahead.": Ibid., page 7.

234 "Something important has just turned up": Ibid., page 8.

235 "Get out of the car": Ibid., page 9.

235 "What's this all about? You're making a big mistake!": Ibid., page 9.

235–36 "The reasons that I did what I did in April of 1985": Aldrich Ames, quoted in the CNN series *The Cold War*, episode 21, March 14, 1999.

236 "The last chapter had been written, the book could be closed": Vernon Loeb, "CIA Still Recuperating from Mole's Aftermath," *Washington Post*, February 22, 1999.

THE CIA SINCE THE END OF THE COLD WAR

254 "intelligence state": John Sipher, "Putin's One Weapon: The 'Intelligence State,'" *New York Times*, February 24, 2019.

GLOSSARY OF KEY ESPIONAGE TECHNIQUES

271 "Each agent's legend, or fictional life history": Harry Rositzke, *CIA's Secret Operations: Espionage, Counterespionage, and Covert Action* (New York: Reader's Digest Press, 1977), page 54.

FOR FURTHER RESEARCH: SELECTED PRIMARY SOURCES

CENTRAL INTELLIGENCE AGENCY MUSEUM
https://www.cia.gov/about-cia/cia-museum

SPY MUSEUM, ONLINE EXHIBITS
https://www.spymuseum.org/exhibition-experiences/online-exhibits

LIVING AT THE NUCLEAR BRINK: A FREE ONLINE COURSE AT STANFORD UNIVERSITY
https://lagunita.stanford.edu/courses/course-v1:MSandE+NuclearBrink
+SelfPaced/about
(requires free registration)

NATIONAL SECURITY ARCHIVE
Able Archer 83
https://nsarchive.gwu.edu/project/able-archer-83-sourcebook
Nuclear Weapons
https://nsarchive.gwu.edu/project/nuclear-vault

THE ROSENBERG ARCHIVE: A HISTORICAL TIMELINE, WILSON CENTER DIGITAL ARCHIVE
https://www.wilsoncenter.org/publication/the-rosenberg-archive-historical
-timeline

COLD WAR INTERNATIONAL HISTORY PROJECT, WILSON CENTER DIGITAL ARCHIVE
https://digitalarchive.wilsoncenter.org/theme/cold-war-history

CENTRAL INTELLIGENCE AGENCY: ON THE FRONT LINES OF THE COLD WAR, DOCUMENTS ON THE INTELLIGENCE WAR IN BERLIN, 1946-1961
https://www.cia.gov/library/center-for-the-study-of-intelligence/csi
-publications/books-and-monographs/on-the-front-lines-of-the-cold-war
-documents-on-the-intelligence-war-in-berlin-1946-to-1961

EISENHOWER PRESIDENTIAL LIBRARY, DOCUMENTS FROM THE U-2 SPY PLANE INCIDENT
https://www.eisenhower.archives.gov/research/online_documents/u2
_incident.html

THE WORLD ON THE BRINK: JOHN F. KENNEDY AND THE CUBAN MISSILE CRISIS, THIRTEEN DAYS IN OCTOBER 1962, JOHN F. KENNEDY LIBRARY AND MUSEUM
https://microsites.jfklibrary.org/cmc

HARVARD KENNEDY SCHOOL BELFER CENTER, CUBAN MISSILE CRISIS
http://www.cubanmissilecrisis.org

FOR FURTHER READING: SELECTED BIBLIOGRAPHY

NONFICTION

Agee, Philip. *Inside the Company: CIA Diary*. New York: Farrar, Straus & Giroux, 1975.

Andrew, Christopher. *The Secret World: A History of Intelligence*. New Haven, CT: Yale University Press, 2018.

Andrew, Christopher, and Vasili Mitrokhin. *The Sword and the Shield: The Mitrokhin Archive and the Secret History of the KGB*. New York: Basic Books, 1999.

Ashley, Clarence. *CIA SpyMaster: Kisevalter, the Agency's Top Case Officer, Who Handled Penkovsky and Popov*. Gretna, LA: Pelican Publishing, 2004.

Bearden, Milt, and James Risen. *The Main Enemy: The Inside Story of the CIA's Final Showdown with the KGB*. New York: Presidio Press, 2004.

Beschloss, Michael. *May-Day: Eisenhower, Khrushchev, and the U-2 Affair*. New York: Harper & Row, 1986.

Bird, Kai. *The Good Spy: The Life and Death of Robert Ames*. New York: Broadway Books, 2012.

Blake, George. *No Other Choice: An Autobiography*. New York: Simon & Schuster, 1991.

Blum, Howard. *In the Enemy's House: The Secret Saga of the FBI Agent and the Code Breaker Who Caught the Russian Spies*. New York: Harper, 2018.

Brimner, Larry Dane. *Blacklisted!: Hollywood, the Cold War, and the First Amendment*. Honesdale, PA: Calkins Creek, 2018.

Cherkashin, Viktor, and Gregory Feifer. *Spy Handler: Memoir of a KGB Officer—The True Story of the Man Who Recruited Robert Hanssen and Aldrich Ames.* New York: Basic Books, 2005.

Cumings, Bruce. *The Korean War: A History.* New York: Modern Library, 2010.

Dobbs, Michael. *One Minute to Midnight: Kennedy, Khrushchev, and Castro on the Brink of Nuclear War.* New York: Vintage, 2009.

Donovan, James B. *Strangers on a Bridge: The Case of Colonel Abel and Francis Gary Powers.* New York: Scribner, 2015.

Dulles, Allen. *The Craft of Intelligence: America's Legendary Spy Master on the Fundamentals of Intelligence Gathering for a Free World.* New York: Lyons Press, 2016.

Duns, Jeremy. *Dead Drop: The True Story of Oleg Penkovsky and the Cold War's Most Dangerous Operation.* New York: Simon & Schuster, 2013.

Gaddis, John L. *The Cold War: A New History.* New York: Penguin Books, 2006.

Gordievsky, Oleg. *Next Stop Execution: The Autobiography of Oleg Gordievsky.* New York: Macmillan, 1995.

Gordin, Michael D. *Red Cloud at Dawn: Truman, Stalin, and the End of the Atomic Monopoly.* New York: Picador, 2010.

Haynes, John Earl. *VENONA: Decoding Soviet Espionage in America.* New Haven, CT: Yale University Press, 2000.

Hoffman, David E. *The Billion Dollar Spy: A True Story of Cold War Espionage and Betrayal.* New York: Basic Books, 2005.

———. *The Dead Hand: The Untold Story of the Cold War Arms Race and Its Dangerous Legacy.* New York: Anchor, 2010.

Howard, Edward Lee. *Safe House: The Compelling Memoirs of the Only CIA Spy to Seek Asylum in Russia.* Washington, DC: National Press Publications, 1995.

Jones, Nate. *Able Archer 83: The Secret History of the NATO Exercise That Almost Triggered Nuclear War.* New York: The New Press, 2016.

Kalugin, Oleg. *Spymaster: My Thirty-Two Years in Intelligence and Espionage Against the West.* New York: Basic Books, 2009.

Kempe, Frederick. *Berlin 1961: Kennedy, Khrushchev, and the Most Dangerous Place on Earth.* New York: Berkley, 2012.

Kessler, Lauren. *Clever Girl: Elizabeth Bentley, The Spy Who Ushered in the McCarthy Era.* New York: Harper, 2002.

Knight, Amy. *Spies Without Cloaks: The KGB's Successors.* Princeton, NJ: Princeton University Press, 1996.

LaFeber, Walter. *America, Russia, and the Cold War, 1945–2006.* New York: McGraw-Hill, 2006.

Lamphere, Robert, with Tom Shachtman. *The FBI-KGB War: A Special Agent's Story.* New York: Random House, 1986.

Leffler, Melvyn. *For the Soul of Mankind: The United States, the Soviet Union, and the Cold War.* New York: Hill and Wang, 2008.

Leffler, Melvyn P., and Odd Arne Westad, eds. *The Cambridge History of the Cold War, Volumes 1–3.* New York: Cambridge University Press, 2012.

Macintyre, Ben. *A Spy Among Friends: Kim Philby and the Great Betrayal.* New York: Broadway Books, 2015.

———. *The Spy and the Traitor: The Greatest Espionage Story of the Cold War.* New York: Crown Books, 2018. ·

Morley, Jefferson. *The Ghost: The Secret Life of CIA Spymaster James Jesus Angleton.* New York: St. Martin's Press, 2017.

Murphy, David, Sergei Kondrachev, and George Bailey. *Battleground Berlin: CIA vs. KGB in the Cold War.* New Haven, CT: Yale University Press, 1997.

Olmsted, Kathryn S. *Red Spy Queen: A Biography of Elizabeth Bentley.* Chapel Hill: University of North Carolina Press, 2002.

Peterson, Martha D. *The Widow Spy: My Journey from the Jungles of Laos to Prison in Moscow.* Wilmington, NC: Red Canary Press, 2012.

Powers, Francis Gary. *Operation Overflight: A Memoir of the U-2 Incident.* Washington, DC: Potomac Books, 2003.

Prados, John. *The Ghosts of Langley: Into the CIA's Heart of Darkness.* New York: The New Press, 2017.

Reel, Monte. *A Brotherhood of Spies: The U-2 and the CIA's Secret War.* New York: Doubleday, 2018.

Rhodes, Richard. *Arsenals of Folly: The Making of the Nuclear Arms Race.* New York: Vintage, 2008.

Richelson, Jeffrey T. *A Century of Spies: Intelligence in the Twentieth Century.* New York: Oxford University Press, 1995.

Rositzke, Harry. *CIA's Secret Operations: Espionage, Counterespionage, and Covert Action*. New York: Reader's Digest, 1977.

Schecter, Jerrold, and Peter S. Deriabin. *The Spy Who Saved the World: How a Soviet Colonel Changed the Course of the Cold War*. New York: Scribner, 1992.

Schrecker, Ellen, *Many Are the Crimes: McCarthyism in America*. New York: Little, Brown and Company, 1998.

Sheinkin, Steve. *Bomb: The Race to Build—and Steal—the World's Most Dangerous Weapon*. New York: Flash Point, 2012.

Stafford, David. *Spies Beneath Berlin*. London: Thistle Publishing, 2013.

Stockton, Bayard. *Flawed Patriot: The Rise and Fall of CIA Legend Bill Harvey*. Washington, DC: Potomac Books, 2006.

Tanenhaus, Sam. *Whittaker Chambers: A Biography*. New York: Modern Library, 1998.

Wallace, Robert, and H. Keith Melton. *Spycraft: The Secret History of the CIA's Spytechs, from Communism to Al-Qaeda*. New York: Dutton, 2008.

Weiner, Tim. *Legacy of Ashes: The History of the CIA*. New York: Anchor, 2008.

Weiner, Tim, David Johnston, and Neil A. Lewis. *Betrayal: The Story of Aldrich Ames, an American Spy*. New York: Random House, 1995.

Westad, Odd Arne, *The Cold War: A World History*. New York: Basic Books, 2017.

Wise, David. *The Spy Who Got Away: The Inside Story of Edward Lee Howard, the Spy Who Betrayed His Country's Secrets and Escaped to Moscow*. New York: Random House, 1988.

Wolf, Markus. *Man Without a Face: The Autobiography of Communism's Greatest Spymaster*. New York: PublicAffairs, 1999.

SELECTED ESPIONAGE AND COLD WAR FICTION

Atkinson, Kate. *Transcription*. New York: Little, Brown, 2018.

Clancy, Tom. *The Cardinal of the Kremlin*. New York: Berkley Books, 2013.

Deighton, Len. *Berlin Game*. New York: Harper, 2010.

Elliott, L. M. *Suspect Red*. New York: Disney-Hyperion, 2017.

Fleming, Ian. *From Russia with Love*. New York: Thomas and Mercer, 2012.

Furst, Alan. *Night Soldiers*. New York: Random House, 2008.

Greene, Graham. *Our Man in Havana*. New York: Penguin Books, 2013.

Ignatius, David. *Agents of Innocence*. New York: W. W. Norton, 1997.

Kanon, Joseph. *Leaving Berlin*. New York: Washington Square Press, 2016.

Kiem, Elizabeth. *Dancer, Daughter, Traitor, Spy*. New York: Soho Teen, 2013.

———. *Hider, Seeker, Secret Keeper*. New York: Soho Teen, 2014.

———. *Orphan, Agent, Prima, Pawn*. New York: Soho Teen, 2017.

LeCarré, John. *The Honorable Schoolboy*. New York: Penguin Books, 2011.

———. *A Legacy of Spies*. New York: Viking, 2017.

———. *Smiley's People*. New York: Penguin Books, 2011.

———. *The Spy Who Came in from the Cold*. New York: Penguin Books, 2013.

———. *Tinker, Tailor, Soldier, Spy*. New York: Penguin Books, 2011.

Littell, Robert. *The Company: A Novel of the CIA*. New York: Penguin Books, 2002.

Mathews, Jason. *Red Sparrow*. New York: Scribner, 2013.

McEwan, Ian. *The Innocent*. New York: Anchor, 1998.

Nielsen, Jennifer. *A Night Divided*. New York: Scholastic, 2015.

Steinhauer, Olen. *The Tourist*. New York: Minotaur Books, 2009.

Wiles, Deborah. *Countdown*. New York: Scholastic, 2010.

INDEX

MARC FAVREAU is an executive editor at The New Press. He is the critically acclaimed author of *Crash: The Great Depression and the Fall and Rise of America* and coeditor (with Ira Berlin and Steven F. Miller) of *Remembering Slavery: African Americans Talk About Their Personal Experiences of Slavery and Emancipation* and the editor of *A People's History of World War II: The World's Most Destructive Conflict, as Told by the People Who Lived Through It*, both published by The New Press. He lives in New York City and Martha's Vineyard, Massachusetts.